RAVENNA MOSAICS

RAVENNA MOSAICS

THE MAUSOLEUM OF GALLA PLACIDIA — THE CATHEDRAL BAPTISTERY
THE ARCHIEPISCOPAL CHAPEL — THE BAPTISTERY OF THE ARIANS
THE BASILICA OF SANT'APOLLINARE NUOVO — THE CHURCH OF SAN VITALE
THE BASILICA OF SANT'APOLLINARE IN CLASSE

TEXT BY GIUSEPPE BOVINI

TRANSLATED BY GIUSTINA SCAGLIA

PHAIDON

First published in Great Britain in 1957 by George Rainbird Limited,
and in the United States of America in 1956 by the New York Graphic Society

This edition published 1978 by Phaidon Press Limited, Littlegate House, St Ebbe's Street, Oxford,
and in the United States of America by E. P. Dutton, New York

ISBN 0 7148 1896 8
Library of Congress Catalog Card Number: 78-56689

*Colour photographs, reproduction, printing and binding by
Amilcare Pizzi SpA, Milan, Italy*

THE EXTRAORDINARY EFFLORESCENCE OF MOSAIC ART IN Ravenna in the fifth and sixth centuries — the Golden Age of the peaceful city on the Adriatic — has left us a great number of mosaics from the early period of Christian art. Neither Rome nor Constantinople nor Salonica can compare with Ravenna, even though many of the Ravenna mosaics have been lost. Its geographical position — the sea was a natural fortification making the city safe from attack — caused Emperor Honorius to transfer the capital of the western Roman empire from Milan to Ravenna in the early fifth century. From that time Ravenna began to acquire the splendour of an imperial city with many magnificent churches and buildings, whose modest brick exteriors gave no hint of the wealth and beauty of the decoration concealed within or of the scintillating splendour of mosaics which covered its walls and cupolas. With the passing of time, many mosaics such as those in the ancient Ursiana, the church of Bishop Peter I in Classe, and in the churches of San Giovanni Evangelista, Santa Croce, Santa Maria Maggiore and Sant'Agata have been completely destroyed. Fortunately, many other structures still retain all their original decoration in fairly good condition, and these are of great importance in tracing the development of Early Christian and Byzantine wall decoration and establishing the stylistic trends of the fifth and sixth centuries.

[5]

It is well known that the nature of the material and the technique employed make ancient mosaics reflect all the light which strikes them. One might even say that light is multiplied because as it strikes the surface it is automatically split into an infinite number of chromatic units — as many as there are tesserae in the mosaic. When one realizes that these tesserae are small cubes, of enamel, glass, marble, and sometimes even of mother-of-pearl, it is easy to understand why an unknown poet, overwhelmed by the dazzling brilliance of light sparkling from the mosaic-covered walls, was inspired to write the following lines which were transcribed on the vestibule walls of the Archiepiscopal Chapel: *Aut lux nata est aut capta hic libera regnat* (Either light was born here or, imprisoned here, it reigns supreme).

In the mosaics of Ravenna, colour and light hold equal supremacy. The mosaic surfaces are areas of sparkling gold, shimmering silver, flashes of garnet, outbursts of emerald green, touches of blue and murmurs of milky white. The whole is such a symphony of colour that Dante, who wrote a large part of his *Divine Comedy* in Ravenna, may well have been inspired by them when he composed the beautiful lines:

> *E vidi lume in forma di riviera*
> *fulvido di fulgor intra due rive*
> *dipinte di mirabil primavera.*
>
> *Di tal fiumana uscivan faville vive*
> *e d'ogni parte si mettean ne' fiori*
> *quasi rubin che oro circoscrive.*

> "And I saw the light in river-form with tide
> Of fulgent fire between two margins streaming,
> Which wondrously with flowers of spring were dyed.

> Out of that current, living sparks were teeming
> And flashing from the flowers with hues intense
> Like very rubies from gold patinas gleaming."

Paradiso 30, 61 ff. Quoted from the translation by Melville Anderson.

In addition to light and colour, rhythm is a third characteristic of the Ravenna mosaics. The figures are more like visions than human beings since they are organized on rhythms resembling the verses of a psalm, giving them uniformity and cadence in general appearance as well as in physiognomy, gestures and costumes. The indivisible elements of light, colour and rhythm give these mosaics still another typical quality: the capacity of the broad surfaces of colour to transform space and dematerialize the architectural structure, producing an intangible halo of atmosphere which varies with the changes of natural light.

[6]

The so-called Mausoleum of Galla Placidia

THE SO-CALLED MAUSOLEUM OF GALLA PLACIDIA

Probably the oldest mosaics in Ravenna are those preserved in a small brick building near the church of San Vitale. It is constructed on a central plan in the form of a Greek cross, with four equal arms, and a rectangular tower over the crossing conceals a dome. Legend has it that it is the burial place of the *Augusta* Galla Placidia, daughter of the Emperor Theodosius. Historians, on the other hand, think that Galla Placidia, who died in Rome in the year 450, was buried in the imperial mausoleum of the Theodosian family. That mausoleum was erected in Rome at the end of the fourth century near the old church of St. Peter's, which was torn down in the sixteenth century and replaced by Michelangelo's basilica. Several mediaeval documents mention a "monastery of St. Lawrence in the region of San Vitale (*monasterium Sancti Laurentii*

[7]

Formosi in regione Sancti Vitalis)" and thus it is conceivable that the chapel in Ravenna was originally built as a small oratory dedicated to Saint Lawrence, the famous Roman martyr so greatly venerated everywhere in antiquity, whose figure occupies a place of honour in the lunette opposite the entrance of the chapel of Galla Placidia. The chapel was not built as an isolated structure, but in all probability, shortly before the middle of the fifth century, it was added to the extreme right narthex of the church of Santa Croce, which once adjoined it. The latter was built by Galla Placidia, sister of the Emperor Honorius, and this explains why the chapel, too, was later thought to be one of the structures built during her reign.

It is clear that the cruciform design of the chapel, which repeats the form of the church of Santa Croce, was selected because it embodies an obvious symbolism whose meaning is expressed in an inscription in the church of San Nazario in Milan: "The church is the form of a cross because it signifies the holy victory of triumphant Christ (*Forma crucis templum est, templum victoria Christi sacra triumphalis signat imago locum*)".

The present proportions of the chapel make it appear lower and flatter than it did originally because the pavement has been raised five feet above the original floor. The plain brick exterior was to be faced with marble, but the rest of the structure was only adorned, as it is today, with a series of blind arcades whose pilasters rest on plinths now concealed below ground. These architectural details give rhythm and variety to the wall surface while the strong cornices and dentils of the triangular pediments of each arm give emphasis to the upper part.

The dimly lighted interior is covered with mosaics and precious marble, the mosaics beginning at a point immediately above the yellow marble-facing added on all the walls in modern times and extending over the whole surface — vaulting, lunettes, cupola and even the mouldings around the windows. Only a few portions of these mosaics have been restored; thus, the complete and harmonious decoration affords a clear idea of the effect that Early Christian mosaics were intended to produce. As light filters softly through the original, small windows of thick alabaster panes and falls on the uneven sparkling surface of the mosaics, the colouristic effect today is precisely the same as it was fifteen hundred years ago. The decoration is extraordinary not only for its colour nuances, but also for its design and subject matter. These qualities inspired the early fifteenth-century humanist, Antonio Traversari, to write "nowhere have we seen a finer or more elegant mosaic decoration (*Musivum nusquam neque tenius, neque elegantius inspeximus*)". In the tenuous half-light of the interior, the basic blue colour scheme would appear even darker, were it not for the myriad reflections of blue and gold that receive the light and create the sparkle.

As one moves to the centre of the chapel, the eyes turn upward instinctively to the dome formed out of high pendentives. The dome is the dome of heaven studded with stars, and around it are the symbols of the Four Evangelists. Particularly expressive is the symbol of St. Mark — a winged lion, whose head is illuminated with white as it emerges from fluffy, iridescent clouds. The deep blue mosaic of the dome is enlivened by the glow of the Latin cross in the centre and by the sparkle of nearly eight hundred gold stars, which swirl around the cross in concentric circles. The cross, as a symbol of the Redemption, has cosmic significance in this setting. As the circles of stars grow narrower, the stars are smaller, thus giving additional height to the dome and increasing the illusion that the sky is receding farther and farther as the eye moves towards the apex. In that quiet, peaceful atmosphere one is reminded of D'Annunzio's words: *grave silenzio per la cupa luce . . . s'ode ora cadere* — "And now in the gloom, deep silence is heard to fall".

The lateral arches directly beneath the dome are emphasized by being decorated with an undulating scroll pattern of dark-blue, light-blue and white tesserae on a garnet-red ground. Within the wall surface of the four arches, pairs of male figures dressed in priestly vestments stand under symbolic, shell-shaped bowers. Each pair of figures flanks a narrow window and their white robes contrast sharply against the dark-blue background, which gradually blends towards green near their feet. As a result, the spectator has the distinct impression that the figures stand on a horizontal plane and that they occupy a place in depth.

These figures are not Prophets, as some have suggested, but Apostles. Among the eight figures one can distinguish St. Peter, who holds in his left hand a key, the traditional attribute of the prince of the Apostles. Both St. Peter and St. Paul can be identified, since iconographic tradition had established their physiognomy by the fifth century. The Apostles point to the cross in the dome with their right hands; at their feet, white doves are silhouetted against the green ground as they walk towards or drink from small, white vessels and fountains, which sprinkle water. These are frequent motifs in classical art, but here they have assumed Christian meaning, the doves symbolizing the good Christians, and the water towards which they walk, the means of attaining everlasting life.

Four of the twelve Apostles were omitted from the arches of the dome because to include them would have required a non-symmetrical distribution. They are represented, however, in pairs on the vaulting of the right and left cross-arms. Elegant paschal candlesticks serve as their base; spiralling flourishes of vine tendrils, growing from a cluster of acanthus leaves, swirl around them. In the centre of the vaulting there are laurel wreaths, which enclose the *chrismon* or monogram of Christ flanked by the Greek letters A and Ω — alpha and omega.

The effect resulting from the technique employed by the fifth-century mosaicists might be termed impressionistic. Though the technique is one which tends to impose strict contours, nevertheless, the artists knew how to model the figures with little touches of white, black or red tesserae; and they knew how to suggest the softness of vines and grape-clusters or the stiffness of acanthus leaves, all of which makes the motifs something more than realistic configurations.

In combining Christ's monogram with the A and Ω, the mosaicist doubtless wished to stress the apocalyptic concept that the Lord is the beginning and end of all things; and it is equally certain that the luxuriant vines and grapes are not mere decorative motifs, but that they, too, are invested with symbolism. It can be no other than the idea expressed in the passage from the Gospel of St. John (15,1): "I am the true vine (*Ego sum vitis vera*)".

The vaulting of the arms on the axis of the chapel was not suitable for a narrative composition; ornamental motifs were used instead and the result is a decoration which is impressively architectonic. The surfaces are covered with a mosaic pattern which resembles an oriental carpet in the way its dark-blue ground is sprinkled with petals of red and white flowers surrounded by gold, white, green, and dark-blue rings, and studded with pale-blue stars and little gold disks. In the whole of Early Christian and Byzantine art there is no decorative motif like it, nor one as beautiful. The only thing comparable to it is a fragmentary Coptic textile of the sixth or seventh century (now in the Egyptian collection of the Museum in Berlin) which shows a similar arrangement of crosses, rings and disks on a blue ground. It is possible that the artist who decorated the chapel may have taken his inspiration from earlier textiles of which this Coptic fragment is a copy.

The arches of the cross-arms are decorated with scintillating, iridescent patterns of various forms: a Greek fret design; a network of green leaves shading to white and trimmed with gold; garlands of red fruit; green leaves spilling out of round baskets woven with gold threads. Placed as they are against a white ground, their brilliance and glow seem to make the cross-arms deeper than they actually are.

The scenes in the lunettes of the cross-arms are almost identical and they are symbolic in character. Against a dark-blue background, two green acanthus tendrils, highlighted with gold, undulate upward in an arabesque pattern, which fills the entire space. They grow beside a small rippling pool surrounded by grass, placed beneath the windows which pierce the lunette area. Two stags leap among the flourishing tendrils towards the water. The stags are, of course, symbolic of the souls crying out to God and were suggested by the psalm: "As the hart panteth after the water brooks, so panteth my soul after thee, O God *(Quemadmodum desiderat cervus ad fontes aquarum, ita desiderat anima mea ad Te, Deus)*".

The subject of the scene in the lunette opposite the entrance is quite different. Under the window there is represented a gridiron being consumed by red flames. On the left stands a small, gold cabinet trimmed with red; its doors being open, we see four books with red bindings on two shelves. They are the four Gospels, inscribed with the names of the Evangelists, Mark, Luke, Matthew and John. On the right, a bearded man, dressed in white robes and carrying a cross and an open book, walks rapidly towards the burning gridiron. The figure has been variously interpreted: some scholars have thought that he is a saint flinging an heretical book on the flames; others have suggested that he is the Christ of the Last Judgment, holding the book in which are recorded the good and bad deeds of all men. The obvious, and undoubtedly the correct, interpretation is that he is the Roman martyr Saint Lawrence. The gridiron is none other than the instrument on which Saint Lawrence was martyred, and is an attribute applicable to him only. He is hurrying towards it because he is eager to give up his life for his faith — *festinat ad martyrium*, to use a favourite expression of the ancient hagiographers — and the Gospel book which he holds symbolizes that faith.

The scene in the lunette directly above the entrance is extremely impressive. A charming, pastoral landscape which glows with the sparkle of yellow and pale-blue tesserae is the setting for the gentle figure of the Good Shepherd, a subject which was popular in the decoration of earlier catacomb walls. Here, however, the symbolism is less obscure than in the catacomb frescoes, for this is very clearly the image of Christ. The shepherd's crook has been replaced by a tall cross; the shepherd's cloak is now a rich gold tunic with a purple mantle over it; and around the head of the Divine Shepherd there is a large, golden halo. There is an expression of incredible tenderness on the youthful, beardless face. An effect of softness is achieved by limiting the number of crimson tesserae in the lighter area of the face and using soft blue for the shaded areas, and by surrounding the face with dark-blond hair, which falls in loose ringlets over the shoulders. Thus, as Toesca observed, the radiance of divinity does not hide his humanity, nor does the ideal figure overshadow the real figure but becomes one with it. Light-blue tesserae rather than gold ones are used for the background and these give the impression that the sky extends into the distance. The majestic figure of Christ, with its long, curvilinear lines, rises against a clear, transparent sky, which seems to cast an early morning light over the whole landscape. He sits on the rock in a three-quarter view, his head slightly turned and his body slightly twisted. His left hand rests on the gold cross, which is thrust like an insignia into the emerald-green meadow; with his right hand he draws towards him, rather than caresses, one of the six lambs standing beside him. The lambs form two groups, three on either side of Christ, and though they are variously posed, they all turn their heads towards him as if spellbound by his presence. Grasses, plants and shrubs soften the rocky landscape and give it rich colour contrasts. The composition is impressive not only for the contrasts of white lambs against the earth-coloured foreground marked by stylized rocks edged with gold, but also by the balanced distribution of the lambs. Though the symmetry is not obvious, nevertheless it is exact insofar as the heads of four lambs are placed so as to echo the curve of the lunette, and all the lines of the composition converge on the figure of Christ.

Seen as a whole, this small, delightful chapel captivates the spectator primarily because the decoration harmonizes so perfectly with the architecture. One of its characteristics is the capacity to give the interior an almost mystic feeling of unlimited space, an effect not found in contemporary Roman mosaics. In the Ravenna mosaics this impression of infinity is created by the gradual blending of colours and the marvellous synthesis of blues and gold in a broad, unbroken expanse. Even when such motifs as white blossoms and figures of Apostles in blue robes are introduced into the vaulted areas, they do not destroy the harmony of decoration and architecture.

A feeling of wonder and mystery overtakes the visitor to this chapel and quite unconsciously his imagination invests the chapel with legendary and dream-world figures. What is particularly surprising is the strange light effects made by the stars in the dome and the downward flourishes of the vines on the cross-arms because, though they are veiled in semi-darkness, they seem to shine with an inner light rather than from reflected light. One is reminded of the words of Venantius Fortunatus, who described the sixth-century mosaics of a church in Paris as decorations "which sparkle with their own rays without the aid of the sun (*Atque suis radiis et sine sole micat*)".

In spite of the small dimensions of the chapel, the mosaics give it monumentality. It has been suggested that the artists who executed these designs came from Constantinople or Syria, but in reality there is no influence from the East. Though some scholars believe that the mosaicists came from Rome, it is entirely possible that they may have come with the court from Milan when the capital of the empire was transferred to Ravenna. Whatever the case may be, it is clear that the iconography of the mosaics in the chapel of Galla Placidia is closely allied to ancient Roman motifs and that the decoration, particularly the Good Shepherd, is unquestionably the work of craftsmen trained in the Hellenistic tradition.

The Baptistery of the Cathedral

The mosaics of the dome

THE BAPTISTERY OF THE CATHEDRAL

The Baptistery of the Orthodox is to be distinguished from the Baptistery of the Arians, also in Ravenna. It is simply the Baptistery belonging to the Cathedral and is sometimes called the Neonian Baptistery in honour of Bishop Neon, who had it decorated about the middle of the fifth century. The date of its construction and subsequent decoration is still very much contested. Andreas Agnellus, the early chronicler of Ravenna and author of the *Liber pontificalis ecclesiae Ravennatis*, states that Bishop Neon had the Baptistery adorned with magnificent representations of the twelve Apostles. Some scholars, however, who base their opinion on the style of the mosaics, maintain that nearly all of the ornament dates back to the time of Bishop Orso, who had been responsible for the construction of the Cathedral. While some historians place the death of Bishop Orso in 396, others maintain that he died some thirty years later, which would seem to be more probable. If the decoration of the dome is dated to Bishop Orso's episcopacy, then the mosaics were executed some decades before the time of Bishop Neon. This would mean that they, rather than the mosaics in the so-called Mausoleum of Galla Placidia, which can be dated shortly before 450, are the oldest preserved in Ravenna. It seems preferable, however, to date the Baptistery mosaics in the time of Bishop Neon, since the statement of Agnellus is very explicit and leaves no room for doubt.

The Baptistery is octagonal in plan, with three projecting apses, and is covered with a dome. The method of constructing the dome is one which Roman architects had used, and consists of inserting two circles of small terracotta tubes into one another, a device which reduces the weight of the dome. The top of the dome was made of pumice stone rather than of terracotta tubes.

In the Baptistery we have another example of a building whose original proportions have been changed. Traces of the original floor were found more than three metres beneath the present pavement, while the remains of a second floor were discovered about 1.75 metres below the present pavement. These facts, together with

[15]

Agnellus' quotation from an inscription in the Baptistery which begins: "Begone, old name, the old must yield to the new (*Cede vetus nomen, novitati cede vetustas*)", have led some scholars to believe that the lowest pavement belongs to an earlier, Roman bath on which Bishop Orso erected a building and that the second pavement was added when Bishop Neon altered the structure. Since the octagonal ground plan was frequently used for Roman baths — though the form is also typical of Christian baptisteries — some scholars believe that the structure was begun as a baptistery, particularly since Bishop Orso would certainly have erected one for his magnificent cathedral.

The brick exterior which we see today is probably not original, but a restoration made in the time of Archbishop Theodore (677-691), considering that the cross on the dome was placed there during his episcopacy; or else it may date from the Romanesque period as the decorative arches of the upper part would lead us to suppose.

That perfect synthesis between architecture and ornament that is so characteristic of the interior of the Chapel of Galla Placidia is also found in the Baptistery. With its surfaces of precious, multicoloured marbles, iridescent mosaics and white stucco reliefs (originally painted with appropriate colours), the total ornament is so closely embedded in the architectural framework that individual structural elements seem to lose all their function and are transformed into pure colour effects. Though the wall decoration consists of five superimposed zones around the octagon and dome, it is composed (and should be viewed) as a rising, vertical scheme which culminates in the medallion at the top of the dome depicting the Baptism of Christ. The beholder's attention is drawn so swiftly to the medallion that his eye does not stop on individual parts. This is because every detail is so closely related to the next and to the design as a whole that the component parts serve their rightful and specific function of coordinating and unifying the light and graceful composition. The fact that no one part of the decoration takes precedence over another does not mean that the decoration is diffused or vague, nor that it is monotonous. If the whole interior is taken in at a glance, one realizes that this system of decoration, which one might feel is lacking in articulation, gives artistic unity to a very well planned structure suggesting the idea of the continuous and the unlimited — an effect that is enhanced by the circular form of the dome.

In contrast to the quiet tonality of the mosaics in the Chapel of Galla Placidia, those of the Baptistery are a symphony of colour which bursts forcefully all over the surface. Bright yellows and greens predominate over the generally light-blue background and occasionally a discordant note of red, violet or white breaks through.

The sides of the octagonal form are spanned by eight wide arches, which rest on eight columns whose bases are concealed beneath the present pavement. Four of the arches are deeper than the others and form apses, originally decorated with mosaics. The mosaics on the spandrels and arches of the lower zone were greatly restored in the nineteenth century. Their backgrounds are of a deep blue, against which lively flourishes of green and gold acanthus tendrils form a spiral pattern growing out of the spandrels, while in the spandrels themselves figures of Prophets are framed within the acanthus tendrils.

In the zone directly above, eight wide arches again span the entire width of each section, but here the arches are articulated by three smaller arches, the central one framing a window. Thus, this zone is effective in making the dome appear less heavy and more spacious. The arches flanking the windows are slightly lower, and within each is represented an edicule or niche with either triangular or rounded pediments. Conventionalized male figures in flat stucco relief are framed within the edicules. The repetition of the arch motif, which emphasizes the rhythm of the pendentives forming the dome, demonstrates the tremendous possibilities that architecture offers to decoration and how much the interaction of these lines helps to give consistency and form to the ornamental whole.

Directly above the window zone two superimposed bands of decoration reach up to the central medallion in the dome, the focal point on which all the ornament converges. In the lower band exotic plants, growing from ample groups of acanthus leaves, continue the vertical rhythm of the eight columns in the lower zones. They separate the series of recessed edicules flanked by narrow, projecting porticoes. In alternate order the edicule has a throne with a cross above it and an altar with the book of the Gospels on it; while in the porticoes there is either a shell niche containing a chair or a tall plant surrounded by a square parapet.

The decoration is entirely symbolic and refers to the omnipotence of Christ, the throne being the symbol either of the *solium regale* of Christ or the judgment seat described in the Apocalypse. The colours glow and vibrate in various degrees of intensity, ranging from the bright chrome-yellow of the portico columns to the cerulean-blue parapet around the plants; from the gold edicules to the purple tones of the cushions; from the various shades of green palms and cypresses to the many light-blue tones blending into grey of acanthus clusters that grow from the spandrels.

There is, of course, an intuitive sense of perspective in the representations of architecture just as there had been in Roman and Hellenistic painting, but on the other hand there is quite a different use of colour — one that is not naturalistic but almost abstract. In addition to the outspoken striving for rhythmic cadences by repetition of forms, there is an entirely new accent and a new spirit in this band of decoration — a quality that forces the spectator's attention by its emphasis on symmetrical compartmentation.

The zone immediately above is not quite as intense in colour. In it Saint Peter and Saint Paul are represented leading the other Apostles in procession and bearing crowns, which are protected from direct contact with the hands by being carried on a cloth. The figures are separated from one another by slender floreate candelabras, which sparkle and seem to flicker like golden rays as they extend elegantly up to the rim of the central medallion. The Apostles proceed slowly over the green ground with uniform gestures and movements that give dignity and solemnity to the scene. The whole is clearly indicative of an entirely new stylistic orientation.

Their gold and silver tunics and mantles are outlined in light blue against the dark-blue sky, a device which brings out all the colours of the garments and makes them blend into the dazzle of the whole composition. It has been noted that the uniform gestures and physiognomies of the Apostles remind one of the never-ending rotation of "eternal wheels" which Dante used to describe the dome of heaven. The head of each Apostle is set against the cascade of a cerulean curtain, which is pulled up to form twelve loops falling from around the rim of the medallion like a gigantic pin-wheel in motion. Richly coloured tesserae are used to define individual features of each Apostle, a characteristic which demonstrates clearly that the mosaicists working in the Baptistery were skilled in portraiture, a feature of Roman art. The head of Saint Peter, for instance, is the head of an old man, but there is nothing hieratic or transcendental about him. Though conscious of his high mission and his authority, he is simply a man of the people. The faces of the other Apostles are not standardized, but show an attempt at portraiture and the mosaicist's interest in the bone structure and planes of the face.

The central medallion depicts the Baptism of Christ. The distribution of the figures and landscape is not particularly well balanced. The mosaic has been largely restored, a fact which is evident in the brighter area of gold in the upper part including the cross, the dove and the heads of Christ and Saint John. Originally, Saint John probably did not hold a patera in his right hand, but rested his hand on Christ's head as he does in the same scene in the Baptistery of the Arians. The simple gold background sets off the rocks of the river-bank with its lovely, iridescent flowers, and emphasizes the transparency of the white and blue water of the Jordan, in which the body of Christ is immersed. A river-god emerges from the waves, carrying in his left hand a green swamp reed (symbol of aquatic divinity) and in his right a green cloth with which to dry Christ's body after the baptism. In later representations of the Baptism the river-god was replaced by angels who hold the cloth.

According to recent studies, the decoration of the dome was planned on the basis of inverted perspective. As a result, the central medallion and the two zones beneath it are to be seen as three successive planes of a single space unit rather than as separate entities. In other words, the scene of the Baptism, with Christ as the central figure and the spectator as an active participant, should be read as having taken place while the Apostles made a triumphant procession around him and in front of thrones and altars placed within the recesses of edicules and porticoes.

Admittedly, there are strong classical elements in this mosaic as there are also typically Roman features in the highly expressive faces of the Apostles, but the work as a whole shows a richness and decorative exuberance which comes close to being Baroque. At the same time, there is a new direction and a new spirit which forecast quite another sort of artistic orientation.

THE ARCHIEPISCOPAL CHAPEL

The Archiepiscopal Chapel stands not far from the Baptistery of the Orthodox near the last remaining tower of one of the ancient city-gates. From the end of the fifth to the beginning of the sixth century it was the private chapel of bishops of Ravenna. Little more than forty years ago traces of the long inscription which Agnellus had transcribed were discovered on the walls of the vestibule. The inscription relates that the little chapel served not only as a repository for relics, of which many are preserved even to this day, but was also used by the bishops to administer the sacrament of penance.

The chapel, dedicated to Saint Andrew, is found on the third floor of a structure whose ground-floor plan is repeated in the other two levels. The building was not erected by Peter Chrysologus, Bishop of Ravenna from 429 to 451, as has been erroneously stated, but by Peter II, who occupied the episcopal throne from 494 to 519 during the reign of Theodoric the Great. The chapel is reached through a small, rectangular vestibule, whose barrel-vaulting is decorated with a mosaic that has been largely restored and completed in tempera. The decoration consists of a pergola formed out of four white lilies growing out of a globe and joined at the tips to small, colourful roses, which are in turn joined to other lilies; between the flowers there are birds of all kinds. The composition closely resembles the decorations on several marble screens in Ravenna where little birds are intermingled with various stylized flowers. The charming colour effect of this mosaic is chiefly due to the contrast of white tones against a gold ground, and white alternating with little green, blue, and purple flowers.

The lunette above the vestibule door depicts Christ as a warrior. The figure, from the waist down, has been restored in tempera and as traces of mosaic were uncovered it was possible to complete the composition and show him in the act of trampling on the heads of a serpent and a lion. The Saviour's head is surrounded by a golden halo, in which there appears a jewelled cross, and his body is clothed in a cuirass under a purple mantle. He stands in a frontal pose with a long cross held against his right shoulder, and in his left hand an open book inscribed with the words: "I am the Way, the Truth, and the Life (*Ego sum via, veritas et vita*)".

The subject of *Christus militans*, the militant Christ, was apparently a favourite one in Ravenna. It was doubtless represented in the destroyed mosaics in the church of Santa Croce, but it is also seen on an Early Christian sarcophagus (preserved under the canopy of Braccioforte and believed to be the tomb of the Prophet Elisha) and in the stucco decoration of the Baptistery of the Orthodox, which antedates the decoration of the Archiepiscopal Chapel by almost fifty years. The scene obviously derives from words of Psalm 90, 13: "Thou shalt walk upon the asp and the basilisk, and thou shalt trample under foot the lion and the dragon (*Super aspidem et basiliscum ambulabis: et conculcabis leonem et draconem*)".

One enters the chapel proper through a door in the centre of the vestibule. The square chapel has the form of a Greek cross with four piers forming arches and supporting a groin vault. Along the ascending line of the vaulting four slender angels in white robes support a medallion in the apex which contains the monogram of Christ formed by the intertwined letters *I* and *X* — the two initials of the name Jesus Christ in Greek. Between the angels, whose white robes make them stand out clearly against the gold background, the symbols of the four Evangelists holding books emerge out of multi-coloured clouds. The angel, symbol of Saint Matthew, is particularly beautiful.

A few isolated portions of the original mosaic have been found in the northern lunette (now decorated with a sixteenth-century fresco) and from these fragments Gerola concluded that in that area there was once a scene with a green ground and a gold background.

In two of the four lateral arches that support the vaulting, the busts of the twelve Apostles are represented in medallions on either side of the bust of Christ as a young man; on the other two arches the busts of six male and six female saints in medallions flank the monogram of Christ. The male saints are intensely austere, an effect which is heightened by their fixed, immobile expressions. The same is true of the women, but they are adorned with jewelled necklaces and on their heads are jewels and silken veils falling behind their shoulders.

On the whole, the colours used are few in number and not sharply contrasted. In fact, the distinguishing feature of the Archiepiscopal Chapel is the simple but extraordinary colour harmony of the mosaics. For the first time in Ravenna we see a gold background being used extensively instead of the traditional blue, but it is clear that the mosaics, from the point of view of iconography, are still rooted in the Roman tradition.

The Baptistery of the Arians

THE BAPTISTERY OF THE ARIANS

The Baptistery of the Arians, built on a small octagonal plan with four apses, was originally surrounded by a heptagonal ambulatory. Its dome is decorated with mosaics similar to those in the Baptistery of the Orthodox. The date of its construction is unknown; all we know is that it was built some time during the reign of Theodoric, and consequently, it may be dated between 493, when that King of the Goths entered Ravenna, and 526, the year of his death.

The artist who created the decoration undoubtedly had the geometric division of Neon's Baptistery in mind, but the much smaller diameter of the dome, built with bricks, hindered him from repeating the decorative scheme of that building. Having outlined the central medallion, he had space for only one ornamental band, whereas the Baptistery of the Cathedral has two.

The central medallion repeats the scene of the Baptism of Christ, with a better balanced distribution of characters. The Baptist here is no longer on the right of Christ, but on his left, and the River Jordan, his head ornamented with two red crayfish claws, emerges completely, instead of half-way, from the waters he

[23]

personifies. The ornamental frieze with the twelve Apostles is also inverted in comparison with the Baptistery of Orthodox. They advance in double procession, bearing gemmed crowns on their hooded hands, and are separated by slender palm-trees, which are no taller than the figures and thus never interrupt their continuous rhythm. Saint Peter and Saint Paul, the file-leaders, carry not a crown, but the keys and a book, and stand at the sides of a great throne, on which a Cross is placed over a red cushion. The Princes of the Apostles meet exactly at the side opposite the Baptism. This, in our opinion, is a grave fault, because one cannot at the same time take in the perspective of the central medallion and the figured frieze around it.

By these variants and by introducing in the circle of the Apostles a throne bearing a Cross studded with gems, the artist tried to avoid giving a slavish imitation of the decoration in Neon's Baptistery; at the same time, for lack of space, the single throne had to serve as the symbol of the judgment seat, which is repeated four times in the Baptistery of the Cathedral. This trend to simplify may be felt in the colour scheme too.

The Baptistery of the Arians does not achieve the intensely dazzling and colourful effects of light and lustre found in the Baptistery of the Orthodox. This undoubtedly is due to a new sense of colour, which led the artist to search for more subdued tones, and to the few dashes of white, since the gleaming enamels were replaced by marble, so much more dull and less brilliant.

The Apostles are all crowned by a cloud and are clad in white mantles. Their movements and draperies are so perfectly similar as to create one single rhythm. Their faces, too, harmonize in this uniformity of design, being all practically alike. Their figures are outlined and clearcut against a background of golden tesserae, which would be just pure light, were it not interrupted by the green stems and leaves of the palm-trees.

Slightly more contrasting colours enliven the central scene. This by no means indicates — as some hold — that this medallion is nearly two centuries later than the frieze representing the procession of the Apostles. Indeed, a technical study has proved the latter to be later, since the tesserae of its edges overlap the central medallion.

The mosaics of the Baptistery of the Arians thus belong all to the same period, even if the Apostles, with the exception of Saint Peter, Saint Paul and the other figure next to him, were executed by a different hand with less artistic skill.

The Baptistery of the Arians

The mosaics of the dome

Sant' Apollinare Nuovo

THE BASILICA OF SANT'APOLLINARE NUOVO

Theodoric had the church which is today called Sant'Apollinare Nuovo built during his reign. This lovely basilica, with its elongated ground-plan, is particularly notable for its many decorative mosaics. Today the mosaics cover only the side walls of the nave, but originally they extended to the apse vault and the inside of the façade, thus endowing the building with a sense of lightness, of not being made of solid matter, through the colour and light reflected in the enamel underlying the mosaic itself.

[26]

The church, erected by the Gothic king near his residence, was at first dedicated to the Redeemer and intended for the Arian cult. Only about forty years later, when the Goths had been driven out of Ravenna, could the basilica be consecrated to the Catholic cult and was then — quite certainly deliberately — dedicated to Saint Martin, the famous Bishop of Tours, considered "a hammer for heretics", *malleus haereticorum*.

About the middle of the ninth century the building housed the remains of St. Appollinaris, the first Bishop of Ravenna; they had been brought from the big basilica of Classe, situated outside the city walls, which was not safe from pirates' raids, quite frequent at the time. On this occasion a semicircular crypt with a corridor running down its middle section was built under the presbytery and the basilica took the name of Sant'Apollinare. It was then called Nuovo (new), probably to distinguish it from the other church of the same name built during the fifth century inside the city walls and called *in Veclo*.

About the year 1000 the right flank of the church front received one of those typical round belfries which, from their shape, may be considered as going back to the Roman wall-turrets containing staircases — and which became typical of the countryside around Ravenna in particular.

Some time later the church — the original floor of which is about 1.20 metres underneath the present one — was furnished with a very wide, deep apse, which during the Baroque period was decorated with stucco-work. Restorations recently carried out and finished in 1951 have restored the ancient building to its original inside dimensions by the building of an apse over the traces of the original perimeter.

The mosaics covering the nave walls consist of three horizontal sections: the first runs along the wide strip of wall between the top of the arches, borne by the double row of columns, and the base of the windows; the second covers the embrasures between the windows; the third is placed between the top of the windows and the ceiling.

Not all these mosaics date from Theodoric's time. The greater part of the lower strip, representing the Martyrs' and Virgins' processions, is later by some decades than the rest, having been executed shortly after the middle of the sixth century, at the time of Archbishop Agnellus, when the church was handed over to the Catholic cult. The style too is clearly different. Indeed, the mosaics belonging to Theodoric's period are still deeply rooted in the Hellenistic and Roman tradition, while those of the Agnellus period are typically Byzantine.

Viewing the mosaics strip by strip, beginning with those which run along the top of the church near the ceiling, they appear as follows:

On the left wall there is a series of thirteen rectangular panels depicting mostly the life and miracles of Christ. They alternate with small ornamental squares showing large shells, the contours of which are shaped like the open wings of an eagle: above, two doves face each other from either side of a Cross. On the right wall a like number of ornamental squares alternating with panels representing scenes of the Passion of Christ form a perfect counterpart to the mosaics on the left wall.

The panels depicting the miracles of Christ contain remarkably few figures, some of which are frequently alike in appearance. Christ, for instance, is always shown as young and beardless, his head encircled by a cloud bearing the Sign of the Cross, while the Apostle who constantly accompanies him frequently raises his right hand in a gesture denoting astonishment at the miracle which is taking place.

The series of scenes starts at the far end of the church, beginning with the first miracle Jesus did, the Water turned into Wine at the marriage in Cana, and ending with the Healing of the Paralytic. Both these panels have been partly restored: the former during the last century was even changed in meaning; the latter, hit direct by an Austrian bomb which fell on the basilica in February 1916, was restored in perfect keeping with the previously existing picture.

The other panels have come down to us well preserved. Among the most interesting and fascinating scenes are the Calling of Peter and Andrew, the Woman of Samaria at the Well, Christ the Judge separating the sheep from the goats, and the Healing of the Paralytic at Capernaum.

In the panel representing the Calling of Peter and Andrew the figure of Christ, although placed off centre, constitutes the axis. In the foreground, on the shores of the sea of Galilee, Christ stands out impressively like a statue. In the middle distance, smaller, a Disciple appears, his white robe offering a perfect colour contrast to the dark one of the Saviour. Three quarters of the picture are taken up by the boat, on which Peter and Andrew stand; they wear short tunics not covering the right shoulder. The former, identified by his white hair and beard, is drawing up the nets, of a lovely greyish rose colour, in which fishes are still threshing about; Andrew, darker-skinned, his hair untidy, is rowing the boat towards the Redeemer. The expression of the two fishermen, more attracted by the eyes than by the gesture of Jesus, shows both astonishment and surprise; indeed the two, at Christ's bidding, fishers of fish no longer, shall from now onwards be *"fishers of men"*. The composition, in which the figures are amply spaced, is enlivened by the dazzling colours blended in the lower part, representing the sea as if in a painting; the waters take on tones of violet, turquoise, green, blue, grey and white, the waves are created by a peculiar arrangement of the tesserae in a curved line, in visible contrast with the regular straight lines of the vast golden background.

The scene of the Woman of Samaria at the well is very simply depicted. The characters are three only: the Woman, Christ and an Apostle. This last figure seems not to take part in the action at all. He could thus be considered of secondary importance: nevertheless, standing behind the figure of Christ, who is dressed as usual in a crimson robe and mantle, he enhances it by contrast with his white robe.

The scene is divided in two by one of the two vertical props sustaining the pulley of the well, which is of a shape quite similar to those still in use today in some parts of the East. On the left the Woman of Samaria, the upper part of her body slightly bent forwards, holds the rope tied to the bucket in both her hands; on the left, Christ is seated not *supra fontem*, as the Evangelist has it (John 4, 6), but on a rocky hillock, at the side of which grows a small tuft of grass. Behind Christ, who is making a gesture as if about to speak, stands a dreamy-faced Apostle, his arm folded over his chest.

The marble rim of the well is quite low, yet high enough for a series of grooves to run down it vertically on the outside. The scene represents this episode of the Gospel in the traditional manner and the way it is laid out recalls some Roman sarcophagi of the beginning of the fifth century. The Christ and the Apostle do not differ much from those of other panels while the Woman of Samaria is extremely spontaneous and vivid: one need only remark her posture and her brilliant shot-red dress, with which the white sleeves of her under-tunic and the small cap she is wearing make a telling contrast.

The scene representing Christ the Judge, rich in light effects, is a subject which differs from the other panels by its inner meaning. The composition is inspired by the Gospel according to St. Matthew where it is said (25, 31 ff.) that *"when the Son of Man shall come in his glory, and all the holy angels with him, then shall he sit upon the throne of his glory: and before him shall be gathered all nations; and he shall separate them one from another, as a shepherd divideth his sheep from the goats: and he shall set the sheep on his right hand, but the goats on the left"*.

In this mosaic Christ does not sit on his throne, but on a rock with white-shot edges; yet the scene is majestic and solemn with the two great angels flanking the Saviour and acting as heavenly guards. The angel on his right has red robes and wings, the one on his left blue robes and wings. These colours belong to traditional symbolism: the angel in red, the colour of light, is the angel of Good, while the one in blue, the colour of darkness, is the angel of Evil. So beside the red angel three sheep in profile, one above the other, signify the Virtuous — indeed Christ holds out his hand to them — while near the blue angel three goats represent the Unrighteous, their coats white no longer but extensively and symbolically spotted with dark-blue markings.

Particularly striking is the mosaic of the Healing of the Paralytic at Capernaum. The sick man, unable to reach Jesus because of the great crowd surrounding him as he preached inside a house, had himself lowered with his bedding through the roof, which was torn away for this purpose.

Christ and the Apostle accompanying him have the same appearance as in the other panels. Completely new, however, is the representation of the most salient moment of the episode although it is not in keeping with the Gospel narrative: the Saviour is represented not inside but outside the house. On the top of the building,

Sant'Apollinare Nuovo

The mosaics on the right wall

now roofless, two men clad in short tunics hold up by ropes the pallet on which the paralytic is lying. The latter, the lower part of his body covered in a red garment, is reaching out his hands confidently towards Jesus, who is moving towards him. This scene, so infrequently found in early Christian art, lacks the balanced composition of the other panels. Perspective is too clearly lacking in the drawing of the house and in the absence of proportion between the figures of Christ and the Apostle and those of the paralytic and the two men at the top of the building. Nevertheless the latter are so lifelike and free that the picture is fully convincing, although it reveals a few serious mistakes if examined in detail: for instance, the fourth rope holding the bed is not tied, yet this was surely done with an artistic purpose to avoid crossing the paralytic's figure by a line which would certainly have marred it.

Most of the panels on the right wall depict the Passion of Christ. Starting from the far end of the church, they begin with the Last Supper and end with the doubt of Saint Thomas.

A great number of characters appear in these scenes, sometimes in groups. There is movement and drama: Christ, older in age, is always represented with a beard.

[31]

This iconographic difference does not necessarily indicate — as has been put forward by some critics — that the left and right wall panels were executed at different times; the style is quite similar in all the panels as can easily be ascertained by comparing the proportions of the figures, the golden backgrounds and the brilliant colour-tones.

The colours, placed side by side with few shades in between, are pure white in the Apostles' robes, amethyst in those of Jesus, and green in the grassy ground. Every now and again there are yellow, blue and dark-red touches, which suddenly change the whole colour effect.

Maybe the artist, by depicting Christ on the left wall as young and beardless, wanted to emphasize his power of working miracles notwithstanding his youthful appearance, while on the right wall he showed him as bearded and middle-aged to underline his human nature, capable of feeling pain. Of particular note on the right wall are the scenes depicting the Last Supper, the Prayer in the Garden, the Kiss of Judas and the Women at the Sepulchre.

In the Last Supper, Christ is seated at the far left of a semicircular dining table. He is surrounded by the Disciples, while Judas sits at the opposite side of the Master. On the table, which is covered with an embroidered, fringed cloth, there are a few loaves and two large fishes on a plate. The feeling of drama is imparted by the expressions of the characters and by the different directions in which they are gazing. While Christ is looking sadly before him, on the verge of uttering the words: "*One of you shall betray me*", Judas, enveloped and gathered inside his white robe, is looking intensely at the Redeemer, but in turn is struck by the disdainful and resentful glances of the seven Disciples nearest him. Only three Apostles, among whom Peter may be recognized, look at Christ in pain and despair.

Symmetry predominates in the representation of Christ praying in the Garden of Gethsemane. The figure of Jesus, his arms lifted wide in prayer, is hieratic, outlined at the top centre of the panel. Six small trees, three on each side, encircle him, rising one above the other from small hillocks on the hilly ground, against a sky of gold. Lower down, on the sides of a grey-green hill, the Apostles are seated, sad and dressed in white, with their heads and bodies in various attitudes inspiring great *pathos*.

In the centre of the panel representing the Kiss of Judas, Christ is solemn and imposing, utterly still like a statue. The face of the traitor, as he approaches Christ to kiss him, is singularly sullen and wicked-looking. At the sides two groups clearly contrast both by their expressed feelings and the colour scheme. On the right, all dressed in white, are the sad and desperate Apostles, although Saint Peter is ready to draw his sword; at the left, but slightly further away, the soldiers stand in gaudy and many-coloured tunics, holding spears, swords and torches. They have just stopped marching and are clearly expecting the highly dramatic event to take place.

In the centre of the panel depicting the Women at the Sepulchre stands the round sepulchre, revealing through its high door the uncovered and empty tomb of Christ. On the left, seated on a boulder, an Angel holds a rod in his hand and gestures as if speaking; his wings are tinged in violet, the nimbus crowning his head gleams with silver. The two Marys are slight and long-limbed; clad in crimson robes and mantles, they come forward with the same movement and gesture. Both their right hands point to the sepulchre, both their faces turned towards the holy messenger seem to question him. Among all the colours of this picture the white of the columns and the bright red of the tomb's roof stand out vividly.

The panels on both walls repeat subjects from the iconographic repertory of typically Roman art. Two of the many scenes are sufficient to prove this point: the Raising of Lazarus and the Foretelling of Saint Peter's Denial. One has the impression of seeing, reproduced in mosaic, one of the many catacomb paintings representing that great miracle of Our Lord, or some of the many sculptures on Christian sarcophagi of the fourth century relating the most humiliating episode in the life of the Prince of Apostles. This consistency with Roman models is of extreme interest, as it proves that Theodoric summoned artists from Rome to ornament the edifices he had built in Ravenna, not from the East, as Cassiodorus relates.

Majestic and solemn figures robed in white garments fill the spaces between the windows, some holding a white parchment, either tightly rolled up, or slightly or even completely unrolled, others carrying a book with a garnet-red cover; they are probably Prophets, not Saints. Although they are differently posed and set so as to look quite different from each other — some are young men in their prime, some middle-aged, some old and showing signs of tiredness in their features, — they nevertheless seem an evenly rhythmic repetition: this is especially due to the fact that they are all represented full-face and follow one another equally spaced and symmetrical on both walls. It is remarkable how the extensive golden background against which these slender figures stand out fails to detract from the solidity of their design or to efface their strong modelling in clearcut contours and subtle shading. The latter clearly show that the artist who created this superb decoration was still fascinated by problems of form and volume.

The mosaics covering the walls beneath the Prophets do not all belong to Theodoric's time. Only the compositions at each end of the two large strips belong to this period: at the near end of the walls, Theodoric's Palace, behind which on one side stand the sacred buildings of Ravenna, on the other the harbour and town of Classe; at the far end, the Saviour enthroned between four angels on one side, the Madonna and Child also between four angels on the other. Today white hangings with touches of colour may be seen between the columns of the *Palatium*; these are not original. They are due to alterations made in Justinian's time, when the Arian church was consecrated to the Catholic cult just after the middle of the sixth century. Some characters were effaced at that time as they were no longer willingly remembered; very probably they were high officials at Theodoric's court, maybe the King himself; the hands of a few are left, half way down the columns, and the semicircular outlines of their heads are still visible. In exactly the same manner the figures originally depicted on the city-walls of Classe were effaced too. But their original contours may be still discerned as the material employed to efface them was different from that of the adjoining undecorated walls.

Over the walls, battlements and towers, buildings may be seen, while on the left on the transparent waters of the Harbour three ships are afloat, one of which is sailing away.

The two mosaics representing Jesus and the Madonna enthroned among angels — partly restored — clearly show a tendency towards greater symmetry: the Redeemer, the Virgin with the Child on her lap, the Angels encircling them, are all perfectly still figures, all placed on the same plane, all in the same frontal position. Impassive, rigid, they seem to gaze fixedly towards some distant ideal point. Lower down, on the emerald-green meadow, the flowers of heaven grow, with white and crimson petals.

The composition is so hieratic and solemn, conceived as it is in a spirit of transcendence, that some critics attribute these two groups not to a follower of the Roman-Hellenistic school, but to some Ravenna-born artist, more easily influenced by the East. In both groupings — as a keen observer once quite rightly pointed out — the artist showed his extremely refined taste in exploiting with great skill the law of contrast between related shapes. Thus he gave the imposing figure of Christ a much greater solemnity by placing tall, lithe Angels beside him, while he spiritualized the mystic figure of the Virgin far more by surrounding her with sturdy, full-bodied

[34]

Seraphs. The artist proved a very knowledgeable expert of expressive values when dealing with form, also in giving a curved shape to the rear columns of the throne where Christ is seated, so that they follow the Redeemer's figure, while the pillars of the narrow throne where the Virgin sits are decidedly vertical, thus stressing the ascending movement of her figure, clad in a crimson mantle with which the white of the Child's robes make a fine contrast.

Just after the middle of the sixth century, when Archbishop Agnellus persuaded Justinian to hand over the Arian church to the Catholic cult, not only did he proceed to efface the characters of King Theodoric's court represented in the mosaics, but he extended this *damnatio memoriae* to those scenes which originally covered the walls between the town of Ravenna and the Redeemer and between the town of Classe and the Madonna. He had these replaced, as the historian Andreas Agnellus of Ravenna tells us, by the procession of Martyrs and the sumptuous train of Virgins, preceded by the Three Kings of the East bearing gifts.

Here the style is quite different: it is the Byzantine style, which Ravenna had adopted some years before, when the apse of San Vitale had been decorated.

There are twenty-six figures of Martyrs, preceded by Saint Martin, the only one clad in an amethyst robe. Clad in white robes and bearing crowns sparkling with gems, all of them, old and young alike, are slowly walking towards the Redeemer over a grassy meadow dotted with white and red flowers; they are all on the same plane and their hieratic gestures and equal rhythm bring to mind the chanting of psalms. Identically shaped slender palms stand between each Martyr and the next, their continuous repetition stressing the recurrent figures on which the whole effect of the composition depends.

This even style is maintained in the faces and garments of all the Martyrs: their features are all depicted by the same weak contrasts in colour, their robes all fall in identical folds. Perhaps the idea of depicting this long procession derives from the friezes of the Apostles in the dome of the Cathedral Baptistery and in the Baptistery of the Arians. Yet the spirit and meaning are different here. The train of the Blessed is moving so slowly as to give the impression that they have even stopped, not to be admired by the faithful going round the Basilica but rather inviting them to move at a processional pace all together towards the far end of the church.

[35]

The whole is too long to be embraced at a glance. The artist had no fear of repeating the same vertical rhythms; indeed he takes pleasure in this motif and repeats it *ad infinitum*, treating the composition as if it were a murmured litany flowing on a single chord. This last effect is achieved by robing all the Saints in identical garments, pure white save for a few ornamental letters on the palliums and the dark *clavi* on the mantles.

Although the elements of this singular composition are constantly repeated, they are never monotonous. The Martyrs have different gestures, poses, draperies and faces. There are marked differences in the way they carry their crowns, in the way their feet are posed slightly apart on the grassy meadow, in their heads, each singularly individual, their robes, the draperies flowing in vertical, oblique, curved or broken lines, with soft or hard, schematic or fluent outlines. There are both harmony and contrast. So each figure stands out, always different from the one nearest it.

Actually it is by such subtle differences that this great master-mosaicist shows his outstanding skill and succeeds in avoiding monotony by simple, shrewd devices, such as the palm branches; these, facing each other, enclose the heads of the Blessed in a kind of ogival arch and seem now completely still, now quivering in a breeze.

Neither does the gold background lack variety; the vast gleaming surface is toned down here and there by some small spot or shade which the mosaicist achieved by putting a few yellowish, pinky or greenish glass cubes among the golden tesserae, or even placing the golden side into the mortar, so that the glass was on the outside and the gold leaf below shimmered through in soft pearly tones.

The line of the Blessed is visually echoed on the opposite wall by the train of Virgins preceded by the Three Kings. Although the Kings were completely restored in the upper part of the body, the variety of colours they must have shown in their sparkling Eastern clothes may still be imagined.

Following the traditional layout of this scene, so common in early Christian art, the Kings are represented in motion, just as, for instance, they are sculptured on the sarcophagus of the Exarch Isacius in the church of San Vitale. Thus they make a contrast with the procession of the Saints who, their heads slightly bent, tread softly, as if weightless, on a meadow strewed with roses and lilies, carrying the symbolic crowns of martyrdom in their hands.

[36]

Like the Martyrs, the Virgins are all in the same posture. Their robes, however, are richly ornamented, quite differently from those of the Martyrs. From the Virgins' high-swept hair long white veils fringed with blue fall over lovely robes made of cloth-of-gold, embroidered with stars, circles and segments in red, green, yellow and brown. On these splendid garments many pearls and gems sparkle and glitter, enriching and ornamenting the hair, neck and belts of the Virgins. Their oval faces enhance their big dreamy eyes, their thin lips are smiling slightly.

Between each figure and the next is a palm, its branches thin and few, and the golden background — of a much paler hue than the one used by Theodoric's artists — throws its iridescent light on the figures, enveloping them in a caress. In this stupendous procession everything is expressed in terms of light, rhythm and colour.

There are twenty-two Virgin Saints, yet they create the impression of being an interminable train. Conceived as a figured litany, each bears her name over her head. All are posed in a similar manner, yet in the details marvellous and surprising differences may be seen: the faces are oval or rounded; the lips are smiling sweetly, yet sometimes tightly closed; the eyes gaze now fixedly, now seem to wonder at some far-off melody; the hair is brown, or black, or again fairer than gold. The gems adorning the elegantly dressed, highly swept hair are as varied as the designs enriching the lovely golden robes. Pearls, amethysts, emeralds and rubies are lavished everywhere. The white of the fabrics is achieved in various tones: the long robes ornamented with *clavi* are depicted by employing enamel tesserae, gleaming with reflected light, suggesting they are silk or damask; the veils over the heads are made with tesserae of rough marble, which tend to absorb, not to reflect light, suggesting wool or linen. Nevertheless the rhythm is always even and the few colours used in contrast, such as in the sandals and in the gem-studded crowns, alternately green and red, never spoil the harmony.

Looking at this superb and melodious train of Virgins, one is reminded of Virgil's words "*Vox omnibus una*".

This impression gains in strength when one realizes that all the figures are designed in curved, soft and flowing lines — a fact suggesting that the artist must have studied the figures directly on a model. A well-known Italian painter recently wrote that in the procession of the Virgins in Sant'Apollinare Nuovo figures may be observed which, although transfigured and unreal as if in a dream, nevertheless are quite like some young women to be met even today in the streets of Ravenna.

[37]

The atmosphere in which these figures live, repeating in quick succession the marked rhythm of the columns beneath them, is but a vast, dazzling dust of gold; not only is the background golden, but robes, hair, clouds, are golden too. Gold against gold, light against light, light itself has become "*sound*"; a light by which, with the continuous repetition of motifs, the whole work of art becomes musical.

The Church of San Vitale

THE CHURCH OF SAN VITALE

The historian Agnellus said of the church of San Vitale: "In architecture and in technical execution there is nothing similar to it in Italy (*Nulla in Italia ecclesia similis est in aedificiis et in mechanicis operibus*)". Though the love for his birthplace may not have permitted him to be entirely objective, and he failed to remember the earlier and similar church of San Lorenzo Maggiore in Milan, Agnellus' admiration for San Vitale is fully justified. Just in construction alone the church is impressive for its daring design; and, in addition, it displays a marvellous synthesis between technical skill and beauty of ornamentation.

Ravenna was still in the hands of the Goths when the church was begun after Bishop Ecclesius returned from a mission to Byzantium with Pope John I, probably after the death of Theodoric the Great in 526. The Bishop appointed Julianus Argentarius

[39]

to direct the construction. A great deal has been written about Julianus Argentarius. Though some scholars consider him to have been the architect of the church and others see him as the "treasurer", he was apparently no more than an ordinary citizen of Ravenna and an extremely wealthy banker. There is reason to believe that he was sent by Justinian on a secret diplomatic mission destined to prepare the way for the Byzantine conquest of Ravenna. But Bishop Ecclesius died suddenly in 534 without seeing the church completed; nor was it completed under his immediate successors, Bishops Ursicinus and Victor. In fact, we know that Bishop Maximian consecrated San Vitale with solemn ceremony in the year 547 or 548 at the latest.

The church is central in plan and octagonal in form. On the brick exterior one sees very clearly that the concentric structure consists of two main forms: a narrow drum fits into a high, broad octagon. The upper portion rises out of the main body very strongly, enclosing and concealing a dome which is covered by a pyramidal roof. The simple, geometric rhythm of the drum impresses us by its clarity of form — a form whose eight smooth sides are articulated by simple, large arches circumscribing the simple lines of the windows.

There is greater articulation in the lower portion, where an ornamental cornice surrounds the structure at a point which indicates the interior subdivision into a two-storeyed ambulatory with windows in both levels. The regularity and monumentality of the octagonal perimeter is broken by a chancel at one side and a narthex at the other. The latter occupies an asymmetrical position with respect to the central axis of the church, a fact which is readily ascertained in the ground-plan.

The interior of San Vitale is particularly impressive for the way eight robust piers extend upward to the full height of the *matroneo* (women's gallery) and form a solid support for the dome. Today the dome is adorned with frescoes executed between 1778 and 1782 by Barozzi, Gandolfi and Guarana. The difficulty involved in completing a structure with a dome was solved with expediency and boldness. The method used was that of inserting terracotta tubes into one another as had been done a century earlier in the Baptistery of the Orthodox. Pilaster strips adorn the eight tall piers connected by arches, through which a two-storeyed ambulatory can be seen. Both the upper and lower ambulatory are further delineated by three smaller arches. The central area receives most light while the ambulatories are shrouded in semi-darkness. As a result, the effect is pictorial rather than sculptural insofar as the openings into the ambulatory tend to dematerialize the solidity of the triple arches which frame them. Space is rhythmically accented by the tall pillars and extend beyond them through the ambulatories. Thus, solids and voids, light and shade alternate in such quick succession that we have the impression of standing in illusionistic and almost dream-like surroundings — a sensation heightened by the natural light which changes with the hour of the day.

The mosaic decoration of San Vitale is centred in the broad, deep chancel. Its glorious symphonic harmony of colour achieves a perfect synthesis between architecture and decoration. The opening to the chancel is marked by a wide and high arch, the underside of which is decorated with fifteen medallions: a bust of the Redeemer in the centre and the twelve Apostles and Saints Gervasius and Protasius (believed to have been the sons of Saint Vitalis) on either side. A wealth of decoration covers the groin vaults of the chancel — decorations which extend to a central medallion in the vaulting and simulate a verdant pergola supported on four struts adorned with garlands. Four angels in white robes are placed in the interstices between the struts and with their upraised arms touch the rim of the medallion. In fact, so emphatic are their gestures that the figures seem to be lifted off the blue globes on which they stand. At the apex of the vaulting the white Lamb of God is framed within a large wreath and set against a blue, nocturnal sky dotted with gold and silver stars. Between the ribs of the vaulting the four sections are decorated with flourishes of green acanthus leaves, which swirl around multicoloured rosettes, stars, birds, animals and fish.

There is a strong feeling of naturalism in the decoration on the right and left walls of the chancel, which have a single theme and, therefore, balance one another. On the arch of the triforium gallery there are doves standing beside large vases out of which vines laden with red and white clusters of grapes swirl around the arch. On both sides of the chancel the vertical posts of the arches contain figures of the Evangelists seated beneath their respective symbols. All four Evangelists wear white robes and all are portrayed as elderly men. On the right wall are Saint Matthew with the angel and Saint Mark with the lion; on the left, Saint John with the eagle and Saint Luke with the ox. The Evangelists are seated in a rocky landscape, which fills the entire rectangular area; their glance is turned upward, awaiting inspiration to compose the sacred gospels.

Beneath their feet the rocks surround pools of water, in which ducks are swimming or tall herons and other birds are standing.

Beneath the triforium gallery is a large lunette framed by an arch. The lunette on the left wall shows two episodes in the life of Abraham: Abraham entertaining the three angels who announce the birth of a child to his wife Sarah; Abraham obeying the divine command to sacrifice his son Isaac but restrained from the act by the hand of God, which reaches down from the sky. The composition is so well balanced and adapted to the curve of the lunette, and so full of feeling, that one recognizes at once the hand of a gifted artist. The entire space is skilfully composed and a balanced arrangement results from the distribution of figures, flowers, rocks, the great oak of Mamre, and clouds. The tall, compact figure of Sarah standing in the door of her hut on the extreme left is in strong contrast to the free gesture of Abraham on the right. His figure, together with the altar and ram, form a pyramidal scheme within the whole composition. In the centre of the lunette the three angels are seated at a table; Abraham has already brought three loaves and is about to serve a dish containing a roast calf. Instead of depicting the figures in strict frontality and with uniform gestures, the artist has made the group more interesting by bending and turning the heads of two angels and varying the position of their hands and feet.

In the arch above the lunette two flying angels hold a wreath which surrounds a jewelled cross. In the left corner the Prophet Jeremiah holds a long scroll as he stands before a low exedra, on which a gold crown has been placed. On the right, a young Moses walks nimbly up the rocks of Mount Sinai to receive the laws. There are reminiscences of modern landscape paintings by Cézanne or Rouault in the way the rocks are stylized and executed in highly imaginative combinations of colour. At the foot of the mountain, the leaders of the thirteen tribes of Israel crowd around Aaron. There are only thirteen persons in this group but it seems like a great crowd because only the tops of the heads of those standing in the back can be seen.

The large lunette on the right also combines two scenes within one composition: the sacrifice of Abel and the offering of Melchizedek. In the centre is an altar, covered first with a gold-embroidered, purple veil, whose transparency permits us to see the four columnar supports; over the veil is spread a white cloth trimmed with embroidery and a tasselled fringe. Two round loaves of bread and a large chalice are placed on the

San Vitale

Interior

altar. Abel, depicted as a shepherd dressed in animal skins and an elegant red cloak, has come out of a rude hut and walks to the altar carrying a small lamb as sacrifice. On the right, the high priest Melchizedek, clad in rich ceremonial robes, has hurried out of a tall temple to the altar with a loaf of bread as offering. Both men look up to the hand of God extended down from the heavens marked by long, reddish clouds. The green earth is dotted with clusters of iridescent flowers and strange plants, which twist and turn to fill empty areas of the composition. Though perhaps slightly inferior in composition to the lunette depicting Abraham, this scene is very expressive and full of movement.

In the framing arch the two flying angels appear again. In the right corner is the Prophet Isaiah and on the left Moses appears twice — once as the guardian of Jethro's flock, seated majestically on a rock, and then on Mount Horeb, removing his sandals before the appearance of God in the burning bush.

Though the wall surface above the arch separating the choir from the apse is very small in area, it, too, is covered with mosaics. Here the artist had to find appropriate motifs which he could adapt to the available space. In the spandrels he placed two palm trees; above the centre of the arch, two flying angels holding a disk with the Greek letter A, from which eight beams of light radiate; on either side of the angels, two green cypresses, and next to them two cities, whose high walls are adorned with many precious stones and thus conform to the description in the apocalyptic vision. The cities represented are Jerusalem and Bethlehem, signifying the church of the Hebrews and the church of the Gentiles, respectively.

In all these lively and colourful scenes in the chancel there is a definite feeling for realism. Though the vivid colours are frequently far from naturalistic, the whole decoration strikes an even balance between design, colour harmony and directness of narrative. Stylistically, all the decoration belongs to the local tradition but is rooted in the naturalism of the Hellenistic school, which clearly did not die out but simply underwent a process of transformation.

In the apse mosaics the style is very different. Here the figures do not bend freely nor do they have volume; instead they are rigid and immobile in a strict frontal position. They do not stand in a landscape filled with atmosphere, but before an unbroken and unreal expanse of gold surface. In this mosaic it is evident that the Byzantine style has reached Ravenna. Its figures are different; its colour is different; and its new subject matter is drawn from a luxurious, cosmopolitan and hierarchical world.

In the half-dome of the apse is represented the young, beardless Christ enthroned on a dark-blue globe. He wears a purple robe trimmed with gold and his head is placed against a jewelled cross set within a halo. On either side stand his heavenly escorts — two angels clad in pure white robes. He holds a scroll with seven seals in his left hand, while with his right he offers the crown of martyrdom to St. Vitalis, who extends his hands under the protection of his elaborate ceremonial robe. Archbishop Ecclesius is represented on the right, wearing pontifical robes. As the man who began the construction of the church, he is appropriately shown holding a model of it — a model whose octagonal form confirms the original plan of the church. The figures stand in the realm of heaven, marked by red and white flowers and two levels of rocks with peacocks and other birds in the lower area. From the rocks beneath the feet of Christ flow the four mystic rivers. The glowing light cast by the broad expanse of gold background invests the figures with a mystic significance that transcends their character as objective images. Some scholars believe that the use of pink-white and blue-white clouds in the upper part of the background is not a Byzantine element, but one that is characteristic of Ravenna.

The two large panels that face each other on the lower apse walls are more specifically Byzantine, and here all the luxury, pomp and splendour of Byzantium as an earthly kingdom is displayed. In the panel on the left the Emperor Justinian, preceded by Bishop Maximian and two priests and followed by civic dignitaries and a group of soldiers, walks slowly forward, carrying a gold paten in his hand. In the opposite panel the Empress Theodora, with the ladies of her court, comes forward bearing a large gold chalice as two courtiers walk before her, one of whom pulls aside a curtain to let her pass through a doorway.

In these panels the artist represented two aspects of the *oblatio Augusti et Augustae* — the presentation of liturgical vessels as imperial gifts — to the church of San Vitale. This is the oldest known representation of the imperial offering made by the Byzantine emperors at Easter time and on other holy days to certain important churches in the city. The practice was continued until the tenth century.

[45]

In the panel depicting the Emperor Justinian, the Byzantine style finds its greatest expression. The moment represented is the one when the procession has paused momentarily and turned to face the audience. The figures, therefore, appear to stand side by side on a single horizontal plane. This frontal view, which is so characteristic of Byzantine art, gives emphasis to the arrangement of colour in broad, simple areas. It should be noted, however, that though each figure when taken individually seems to be static and arrested in motion, the group as a whole appears to move slowly towards the right. This effect is achieved simply by aligning the forearms of all the men in a horizontal position, but then giving the forearm of the deacon carrying the missal a slight downward angle and an even stronger downward thrust to the arm of the sub-deacon holding an incense-burner. The broad colour areas of the garments make the figures appear stiff and flat, as though no real body existed beneath the robes. Despite the definite attempt at portraiture in some of the heads, they impress us as figures belonging in an unreal world that exists beyond time and space.

Bishop Maximian was ordained by Pope Vigilius on the 14th of October, 546, at Patras in Achaea and from there he was sent to Ravenna. He seems to occupy a prominent position in the group not only because he is placed more in the foreground but also because his head has more space on either side than do the others. He is, furthermore, the only one whose name is inscribed over his head. He wears the robes of a bishop and carries a jewelled cross, symbol of his sacred authority. His strongly delineated features and penetrating blue eyes suggest a man of uncompromising character and keen intelligence. The mosaic must have been very familiar to Agnellus since it fits his description of Maximian as: "Tall in stature, slender in body, lean in face, bald-headed but for a few hairs, grey-eyed, and saintly in character (*Longeva statura, tenui corpore, macilentus in facie, calvus capite, modicos habuit capillos, oculos glaucos et omni gratia decoratus*)".

The head of Justinian, with its straight, slender nose and large, staring eyes under the dark, strongly arched eyebrows, was probably copied from the imperial medals which were distributed throughout the Byzantine provinces. He dominates the centre of the composition and is distinguished from the others not only by his purple mantle, crown and halo, but also because at no point do the robes of the men flanking him overlap his own. In the way the hem of his mantle is drawn up and pulled back slightly, there seems to be an intentional attempt to set him apart from the rest and not let his mantle intrude on the silhouette of Maximian's figure. All the other figures in the mosaic

San Vitale

The mosaics of the presbytery

occupy a secondary plane and in no way come forward. In fact, there are really only two prominent figures in the panel: the Emperor as the *regalis potestas* and the Archbishop Maximian as the *sacra auctoritas*.

The mosaic on the opposite wall, which portrays the Empress Theodora, is much richer in colour. White and purple are used extensively and many other colours are variously juxtaposed to make a vibrant and intense colour harmony. The tall, slender Empress wears a large mantle trimmed with gold embroidery, a splendid jewelled necklace around her shoulders and a magnificent crown. A large golden halo, symbol of the power invested in her by God, scintillates behind her head. Every detail, including the tiny face, is calculated to emphasize her royal heritage and position. The horizontal position of her arms and hands, which hold the jewelled chalice, is forcefully stressed as if she were urging the ladies of her court to proceed behind her towards the door on the left. The ladies, who are smaller in stature than the Empress, have stopped and stand in a line facing front. But this seems to be only a momentary

[47]

pause, for the impression is that they will move on at once as the courtier pulls aside the brightly decorated curtain on the doorway to let the Empress enter. Theodora at this moment stands before a shell-shaped apse decorated with pearl garlands outlined against the rhythmic pattern of the green half-dome. In contrast to the five women in the right corner, who have stereotyped features making them all look alike, the two ladies nearest the Empress bear a certain resemblance to each other. It has been suggested that they are Antonina, the wife of the general Belisarius, who captured Ravenna from the Byzantines in the year 540, and her daughter Johannina, whom Procopius mentions as a close friend of Theodora.

The plastic forms and illusionistic depth which had characterized the style of the earlier Ravenna mosaics is no longer evident in these two panels. The modelling in light and shade has been abandoned, and realistic figures have given way to purely decorative abstractions. The figures have been converted into rhythmic lines and shapes like the counterpoint of a musical score, and the gem-like colour rises to a supreme pitch — an effect created by the richness of material, which casts light and reflections not only from the infinite number of glass tesserae, but also from innumerable touches of mother-of-pearl. Once these two panels had been finished the decoration of San Vitale was complete. Here in the chancel of the church, surrounded by the splendour of iridescent mosaics, we are completely captivated and drawn into the mysterious spell of the Orient.

Sant'Apollinare in Classe

SANT'APOLLINARE IN CLASSE

The building of the magnificent basilica of Sant'Apollinare in Classe outside the city walls was initiated by Bishop Ursicinus, but he did not live to see it completed, for he died in 536 after only three years in office. Like San Vitale, it was built at the expense of the banker Julianus Argentarius and consecrated by Bishop Maximian, one of the most intelligent and active Archbishops of Ravenna. The ceremony took place in all solemnity — as we know from historical sources — on the ninth of May of the year 549. Majestic and solemn, its background seawards that dark-green age-old pine wood sung by Dante and Byron, the basilica is about 4 km. south-east of Ravenna, overlooking the former swamp, today converted by the industrious labour of man into a large fertile stretch of land.

Those coming from afar are struck at first glance by the imposing structure with its solid, powerful belfry, towering 37.50 metres above one side of the church. It is

[49]

one of those round belfries typical of the countryside around Ravenna, built may be near the end of the tenth century, with material taken from other buildings; the upward series of mullioned windows with one, two and three lights, ornamented with little columns bearing crutch-shaped capitals, makes the belfry appear more elegant and slender.

The basilica was built near the famous harbour of Classe, which Augustus had equipped with a powerful navy to defend the *Mare Supernum* and the seas of the Near East. Saint Apollinaris, who was — according to Saint Peter Chrysologus — the first Bishop of Ravenna, brought word of the Gospel and the new faith to the population of the *castrum classense*, made up mostly of merchants and soldiers enlisted in different parts, sometimes very distant, of the Empire. The period in which the Bishop lived is not known; in any case it is difficult to believe he was a contemporary of the Apostles, as the *"Passio S. Apollinaris"*, a legendary tale written possibly in the sixth century, would have it. Evidently the writer had a dual purpose in going back to such ancient times: first to ennoble the figure of the first Bishop of Ravenna and secondly to enhance the importance and authority of the church of Ravenna.

The earthly remains of St. Apollinaris were buried in one of the cemeteries built near the *oppidum* of Classe, in an underground stone ark. The great basilica was built right beside the tomb, its size 55.58 by 30.30 metres; its extremely simple architectural lines give the vast interior a solemn, impressive atmosphere.

Twenty-four beautiful marble columns, topped by capitals ornamented with acanthus leaves — curved outwards as if bowed by a wind coming from within the capitals themselves — divide the space into three naves. Daylight pours in through forty-eight side windows and five in the apse.

The walls are today bare and unadorned and show but a surface of rose-coloured bricks; originally however, they were all covered with precious marbles and must have reflected the light like mirrors. This Andreas Agnellus, the historian of ninth-century Ravenna, tells us, adding that no basilica in Italy was equal to this one *"in lapidibus preciosis"*.

Perhaps it was this extraordinary wealth of marbles which induced Sigismondo Malatesta, lord of Rimini, in the fifteenth century, to ask permission to remove most of the costly material; he used it to transform and embellish the church of San Francesco in Rimini, a task he entrusted to Leon Battista Alberti and other Renaissance artists.

The presbytery of San Vitale today is on a much higher level, because a ring-shaped crypt was added towards the end of the ninth century, maybe at the time of Archbishop Dominicus Ublatella (889-898), who is known to have rebuilt the high altar and consequently the presbytery too. At the time the basilica was built, the site of this presbytery was occupied by the *bema*, the place reserved for the clergy, which extended towards the centre of the building, reaching as far as the three last columns from the far end. Its foundations, on which the transoms and the small marble pillars compassing it stood, were discovered in 1953, only thirty centimetres beneath the present flooring.

This is an interesting discovery, not only because it is the first example of this kind proved to have existed in Ravenna, but also because its existence provides a link with Eastern architecture. Other such links may be seen in the *diaconicon* and the *prothesis* flanking the apse, the many side-doors of the basilica, and the two turrets which at one time rose at the far end of the *pronaos* (porch). The *pronaos* itself had four sides, as was established by excavations carried out during the last century.

Of the ancient mosaics which must have covered the whole floor of the church like one immense carpet, only a few remains are left: a piece in geometrical design still bears an inscription, near the beginning of the right aisle, stating how much of the surface one *Gaudentia* and one *Felix*, together with other donors, had covered in mosaic at their expense; another small bit of flooring, found under the pavement of the right aisle, was detached in 1953 and is now against the south wall of the church.

Along the aisles there is a series of sarcophagi dating from the fifth to the ninth century. They are sculptured, especially on the front and top, sometimes on all four sides, showing either scenes with figures or simple geometrical and symbolic designs, and have characteristic covers which are either rounded or roof-shaped. In some of these sarcophagi valuable materials were found in 1949, including a crimson-coloured silk veil and fragments of episcopal girdles bearing inscriptions in uncial characters, ascribed to the end of the seventh or the beginning of the eighth century.

As one enters the basilica of Classe, the eye is immediately caught and held by the vast mosaics covering the apse vault and its arch like a rich coloured cloak. The colours are very varied and abstract symbols abound.

The mosaics do not all belong to the same period. Those of the apse vault, the four Bishops between the windows, and the two palms and the two archangels on the sides of the arch are earlier than the second half of the sixth century; the historical and symbolic scenes in the lower part of the apse belong to the second half of the seventh century; the top of the arch was decorated in the seventh century according to a few critics, but more probably in the ninth; the two half-figures of Apostles or Evangelists at the bottom date from the tenth or eleventh century.

At the centre of the highest part of the arch a bust of Christ is depicted inside a round medallion on a yellowy pinkish ground made of tesserae which are no longer of vitreous composition. Lean-faced and bearded, crowned by a golden cloud and bearing a Cross, the Saviour holds a book in his left hand and imparts a blessing with his right. The symbols of the four Evangelists are beside him, all half-figures on a dark-blue background, emerging from a conventionally elongated bank of blue and red clouds. Among these winged, cloud-surrounded symbols, Saint Luke, represented as a calf on the far right, is of particular interest: although the head is drawn completely in profile, both nostrils appear as if seen from the front. This detail may recall some of Picasso's drawings, a thousand years later!

Beneath this wide rectangular strip, edged below by a narrow mosaic border, twelve white sheep — the Apostles — six on each side, are represented as having come out, one after the other, from the gem-studded walls of the towns of Jerusalem and Bethlehem, symbolizing the Church of the Hebrews and the Church of the Gentiles. Against the golden sky, in which the usual clouds are symmetrically outlined, the twelve sheep climb a green hill, which goes right up to the top of the arch. In these two mosaics the colour tones are nearly all flat, so the figures take on their particular value only by their marked contour lines.

Lower down, on the sides of the arch, against a dark-blue background, there are two golden-green palms with thin trunks and widely spread branches, bearing brilliant red fruit hanging in bunches.

Still lower down are depicted the practically identical figures of the Archangels Michael and Gabriel. They are represented as holy standard-bearers, wearing rich military garments and carrying a banner, on which the Greek words praising God as "Holy, holy, holy" may thus be read: ΑΓΙΟC, ΑΓΙΟC, ΑΓΙΟC. Under the dais where the two Archangels stand lilies and roses grow: these are the flowers of the garden of Heaven. They are similar to the flowers in the green meadows depicted, may be by the same mosaicists, in the apses of San Michele in Africisco and San Vitale.

Sant' Apollinare in Classe

The Centre Nave

The great arch ends at the bottom with two small panels in much quieter colours, white and grey predominating. Either two Apostles or two Evangelists are represented: one is identified by the inscription MATHEVS. The dry-cut design would appear to place these figures in about the year one thousand. The mosaics at the bottom of the sides of the apse are similar to those of San Vitale in subject, but the colours are quieter and have less warmth and brilliance.

The remains of the left panel date back to the time of Archbishop Reparatus (671-677). It represents the Emperor of the East, Constantine IV Pogonatus and his brothers Heraclius and Tiberius entrusting deeds to the Church of Ravenna, thus making it independent from the Church of Rome; for this reason Archbishop Maurus and his legate Reparatus, who strenuously sustained the independence of the Church of Ravenna, are included in the picture. Unluckily the panel was much restored and consists today mostly of tempera simulating mosaic. The heads too were greatly restored and no longer belong to seventh-century art. Even in the original pieces the modelling

[53]

is rather poor and the artist evidently tried to make up for lack of art by robing the figures in extremely sumptuous garments.

The panel opposite is of a mystic nature and depicts the sacrifices of Abel, Melchizedek and Abraham. The general plan recalls similar mosaics in the presbytery of San Vitale, but here three scenes are combined in one composition. The panel does not lack a certain balance, but the design is no longer fluent and the lines lack softness; the colour, achieved by tesserae of a material different from enamel, is not luminous.

In the spaces between the windows bishops Ursicinus, Ursus, Severus and Ecclesius are represented, all in similar fashion inside recesses overhung by a shell; clad in his liturgical vestment, each holds a sacred book in his left hand, covered by the chasuble. Their bodies are rather flat, yet their faces have some expression: this is due in particular to the way the lines of tesserae follow the face muscles. The figure of the founder, Ursicinus, is particularly striking from this point of view, his features are so vivid as to be a real portrait.

The great vault of the apse, in which a few brilliant yet harmonious colours are used, bears a partly symbolic, partly descriptive scene on the upper part. Right at the top, on a golden sky background, the Hand of God and the two half-figures of Elijah and Moses emerge from elongated reddish clouds. The two Prophets are symmetrically placed at the sides of the great central medallion studded with gems. Among the myriads of stars in the medallion is a great Cross; the face of Christ is depicted in its centre. Slightly lower down on the green meadow stand three lambs, looking in ecstasy towards the medallion. The composition clearly represents the Transfiguration of Christ on Mount Tabor: this is confirmed by the presence of Moses and Elijah, and of the three lambs, symbolizing the three Apostles — Peter, James, John — who, according to the Gospel, were present. The lower part of the picture shows a wide expanse of green ground on which small brown or yellow-green rocks edged in white or blue alternate with flowers, plants, grasses and trees of different kinds; the pine-tree, even today typical of the countryside around Classe, is clearly recognizable. A fresh, enchanting naïvety springs from the whole composition, in which full and empty spaces are very harmoniously placed, thus creating a perfect balance of masses.

At the centre of this green flowery vault, enlivened by some birds, the hieratic figure of Saint Apollinaris stands with his hands wide apart and uplifted in a gesture of prayer. On each side of him six white sheep are approaching along a path bestrewed with wild roses and small flowering lilies: they symbolically represent the faithful entrusted to the care of the Saint as the Shepherd. Here inspiration was surely taken from the last words of Saint Peter Chrysologus' sermon in honour of the First Bishop: "*Ecce vivit, ecce ut bonus pastor suo medio assistit in grege*"; behold He lives, behold like a good shepherd he stands amid his flock.

With the decoration of Sant'Apollinare in Classe the series of mosaics preserved in Ravenna ends. As we have seen, they comprise works of different styles, Roman-Hellenistic, Ravenna and Byzantine. Mosaics which make different impressions on different people, but no-one can fail to marvel how the colours seem to live and breathe. On these surfaces light does not fall in a beam as in a mirror, but is diffracted into as many parts as there are tesserae, and these, having been set by the mosaicist at varying angles, create a multitude of chromatic effects. So, as the onlooker moves along, the tesserae light up or die down, sparkle or vanish, shimmering continuously and creating the impression of something changing, vital, alive.

BIBLIOGRAPHY

THE SO-CALLED MAUSOLEUM OF GALLA PLACIDIA

X. Barbier de Montault, Eglise de St. Nazaire (vers 449?), in *Revue de l'Art Chrétien*, 1896, p. 177-188.

H. Duetschke, Das Laurentiusmosaik der Galla Placidia, in *Ravennatische Studien*, Leipzig, 1919, p. 265-274.

S. Ghigi, *Il Mausoleo di Galla Placidia in Ravenna*, Bergamo, 1910.

E. Bottini-Massa, *I musaici di Galla Placidia a Ravenna — Saggio di una nuova interpretazione*, Forlì, 1911. (*cf.* the article in *Felix Ravenna*, 1912, p. 260-264).

C. Ricci, Il sepolcro di Galla Placidia in Ravenna, in *Bollettino d'Arte*, 1914, p. 141-174.

E. Bottini-Massa, L'Oratorio di Galla Placidia e la 'ecclesia Sanctae Crucis' del Liber Pontificalis Ravennate: studio sulla identificazione del monumento e il simbolismo della decorazione musiva, in *La Romagna*, 1923.

F. Filippini, La vera interpretazione dei musaici del Mausoleo di Galla Placidia in Ravenna, in *Atti e Memorie della Deputazione di storia patria per la Romagna*, IV, ser. XIII, 1923, p. 187-212.

A. Testi-Rasponi, Il 'monasterium Sancti Laurentii Formosi' di Ravenna, in *L'Arte*, XXVIII, 1925, p. 71-76.

C. Ricci, *Tavole storiche dei musaici di Ravenna, I, Sepolcro di Galla Placidia*, Roma, 1930.

F. Filippini, Il valore simbolico dei musaici del 'Mausoleo' di Galla Placidia in Ravenna, in *Bollettino d'Arte*, 1931, p. 367-375. (Cf. the article by S. Muratori in *Felix Ravenna*, 1931, p. 65-68).

J. Zeiller, Sur une mosaique du Mausolée de Galla Placidia à Ravenne, in *Comptes-Rendus de l'Académie des Inscriptions et Belles Lettres*, 1934, p. 43-53.

W. Seson, Le jugement dernier au Mausolée de Galla Placidia, in *Cahiers Archéologiques*, Paris, I, 1945, p. 37-50 (Cf. the article by G. Bovini in *Felix Ravenna*, I, 1950, p. 64-67).

P. Courcelle, Le gril de Saint Laurent au Mausolée de Galla Placidia, in *Cahiers Archéologiques*, III, 1948, p. 29-39.

G. Bovini, *Il cosidetto Mausoleo di Galla Placidia in Ravenna*, Città del Vaticano, 1950, p. 104.

THE BAPTISTERY OF THE CATHEDRAL

X. Barbier de Montault, Baptistère de la Cathédrale (449-452), in *Revue de l'Art Chrétien*, 1896, p. 73-86.

C. Ricci, Il Battistero di S. Giovanni in Fonte, in *Atti e Memorie della R. Deputazione di Storia Patria per la Romagna*, Ser. III, Vol. VII, Bologna, 1889.

C. Sangiorgi, *Il Battistero della Basilica Ursiana di Ravenna*, Ravenna, 1900.

J. Ficker, Der Bildschmuck des Baptisterium Ursianum in Ravenna, in *Byz. Neugr. Jahrb.*, II, 1921, p. 319-328.

C. Ricci, *Tavole storiche dei musaici di Ravenna; II; Il Battistero della Cattedrale*, Roma, 1931.

S. Bettini, Il Battistero della Cattedrale, in *Felix Ravenna*, 1950, I, p. 41-59.

THE ARCHIEPISCOPAL CHAPEL

X. Barbier de Montault, Chapelle de l'Archevêché, in *Revue de l'Art Chrétien*, 1896, p. 275-284.

G. Gerola, Il ripristino della Cappella di S. Andrea nel Palazzo Vescovile di Ravenna, in *Felix Ravenna*, 1932, II, p. 71-132.

C. Ricci, *Tavole storiche dei musaici di Ravenna, V: La cappella arcivescovile (Oratorio di S. Andrea)*, Roma, 1934.

THE BAPTISTERY OF THE ARIANS

X. Barbier de Montault, Eglise de Ste Maria-in-Cosmedin, in *Revue d'Art Chrétien*, 1896, p. 284-291.

S. Ghigi, Il Battistero degli Ariani in Ravenna (sec. VI), in *Atti e Memorie della R. Deputazione di Storia Patria per la Romagna*, Series IV, 1915, VI, p. 278-315.

G. Gerola, *Il restauro del Battistero Ariano di Ravenna*, in *Studien zur Kunst des Ostens*, Leipzig, 1923, p. 112-129.

C. Ricci, Il Giordano del Battistero degli Ariani, in *Felix Ravenna*, 1929, fasc. 33, p. 1-6.

C. Ricci, *Tavole storiche dei mosaici di Ravenna, III, Il Battistero degli Ariani*, Rome, 1932.

SANT'APOLLINARE NUOVO

X. Barbier de Montault, Eglise St-Apollinare-le-Neuf (VI° siècle), in *Revue de l'Art Chrétien*, 1896, p. 459-484.

C. Ricci, Le nozze di Cana (Mosaici del VII secolo in Sant' Apollinare Nuovo di Ravenna), in *Rassegna d'Arte*, I, 1901, p. 19-20.

C. Ricci, La vita di Gesù (Mosaici del VI secolo) in *Emporium*, XV, Bergamo, 1902, n. 88, p. 261-284.

A. Baumstark, I Mosaici di Sant'Apollinare Nuovo e l'antico anno liturgico ravennate, in *Rassegna Gregoriana*, IX 1-2, Rome, 1910.

G. Galassi, Le Vergini di Sant'Apollinare Nuovo (Valutazione estetica) in *Felix Ravenna*, 2nd Suppl., 1916, p. 99-110.

F. Lanzoni, Studi storico-liturgici su Sant'Apollinare Nuovo, in *Felix Ravenna*, 2nd Suppl., 1916, p. 56-74.

S. Muratori, Di alcuni restauri fatti e da farsi nei mosaici di Sant'Apollinare Nuovo, in *Felix Ravenna*, 2nd Suppl. 1916, p. 56-74.

C. Ricci, Per la storia di Sant'Apollinare Nuovo, II, I mosaici, in *Felix Ravenna*, 2nd Suppl., 1916, p. 39-43.

F. di Pietro, Un quesito stilistico nei mosaici di Sant'Apollinare Nuovo, in *Bollettino del R. Liceo-Ginnasio Dante Alighieri*, Ravenna 1925-26 (publ. 1927), p. 11-15.

R. Delbrueck, Mosaik-Darstellung des Theoderich-Palastes in Sant'Apollinare Nuovo, in *Bollettino dell'Associazione Internazionale di Studi Mediterranei*, I n. 1.

R. Bartoccini, Sondaggi nei mosaici teodoriciani di Sant'Apollinare Nuovo in Ravenna, in *Felix Ravenna*, 1932, 2nd. issue, p. 168-170.

C. Ricci, *Tavole storiche dei mosaici di Ravenna*, IV, *Sant'Apollinare Nuovo*, Roma, 1933.

Fr. von Lorentz Theodorich, nicht Justinian, in *Römische Mitteilungen*, 50, 1935, p. 339-347.

E. Dyggve, Ravennatum Palatium sacrum: la basilica ipetrale per cerimonie, in *Det kgl. Danske Videns-kunsthistoriske kabernes Selskab - Archaeologisk Meddelelser*, III, 2, Copenhagen, 1941.

G. Bovini, L'ultimo pannello musivo della parete sinistra della chiesa di Sant'Apollinare Nuovo in Ravenna ed il problema del suo restauro, in *Felix Ravenna*, 1950, 2nd issue, p. 20-39.

G. Bovini, Oros bizantinos sobre la orilla del Adriatico, in *Histonium, Buenos Aires*, 1951, n. 141, p. 50-51.

G. Bovini, L'aspetto primitivo del mosaico teodoriciano raffigurante la "Civitas Classis" in Sant'Apollinare Nuovo, in *Felix Ravenna*, 1951, 4th issue, p. 57-62.

G. Bovini, Nuove constatazioni sulla tecnica e sui mosaici di Sant'Apollinare Nuovo di Ravenna, in *Atti del I Congresso Nazionale di Archeologia Cristiana* (Siracusa 1950), Rome, 1952, p. 101-106.

G. Bovini, Osservazioni sul frontone del "Palatium" di Teodorico figurato nel mosaico di Sant'Apollinare Nuovo di Ravenna, in *Beiträge zur älteren europäischen Kulturgeschichte, I, Festschrift für Rudolf Egger*, Klagenfurt, 1952, p. 206-211.

G. Bovini, Una prova di carattere tecnico dell'appartenenza al ciclo iconografico teodoriciano della Madonna in trono, figurata sui mosaici di Sant'Apollinare Nuovo a Ravenna, in *Studi Romagnoli*, III, 1952, p. 19-26.

G. Bovini, Nuovissime osservazioni sulla tecnica e sui mosaici di Sant'Apollinare Nuovo a Ravenna, in *Atti dell' VIII Congresso Internazionale di Studi Bizantini*, II, Roma, 1953, p. 96-99.

L. B. Ottolenghi, I Profeti ed i Santi nei mosaici della Basilica di Sant'Apollinare Nuovo, in *Bollettino Economico della Camera di Commercio Industria e Agricoltura di Ravenna*, 1954, n. 11 p. 6-7.

THE CHURCH OF SAN VITALE

X. Barbier de Montault, Eglise St. Vital (de 534 à 547), in *Revue de l'Art Chrétien*, 1896, p. 22-46.

J. Quitt, Der Mosaiken-Zyklus von S. Vitale in Ravenna; Eine Apologie des Dyophysitismus aus dem VI Jahrhundert, in *Byzantinische Denkmäler*, III, 1903, p. 71-109.

C. Ricci, *Tavole storiche dei musaici di Ravenna*, VI: *S. Vitale*, Roma, 1935.

S. Bettini, *Die Mosaiken von S. Vitale in Ravenna*, Berlin, 1940.

S. Muratori, *I mosaici di S. Vitale*, Bergamo, I ed., 1942; II ed., 1945.

G. Rodenwaldt, Bemerkungen zu den Kaisermosaiken in S. Vitale, in *Jahrbuch des deutschen archäologischen Instituts*, 59-60, 1945-46 (1949), p. 88-110.

C. Cecchelli, Le 'imagines' imperiali in S. Vitale, in *Felix Ravenna*, 54, 1950, p. 5-13.

F. W. Deichmann, Contributi all'iconografia e al significato storico dei mosaici imperiali in S. Vitale, in *Felix Ravenna*, 60, 1952, p. 5-13.

P. Toesca, *S. Vitale di Ravenna — I mosaici*, Milano, 1952.

SANT'APOLLINARE IN CLASSE

X. Barbier de Montault, Eglise Sant'Apollinare in Classe, in *Revue de l'Art Chrétien*, 1896, p. 363-385.

G. Galassi, La cosi detta decadenza nell'arte musiva ravennate: i mosaici di Sant'Apollinare in Classe, in *Felix Ravenna*, 1914, 15th issue, p. 623-633; 15th issue p. 683-691.

G. Gerola, Quadro storico nei mosaici di Sant'Apollinare in Classe, in *Atti e Memorie della Deputazione di Storia Patria per le Provincie della Romagna*, IV series VI, 1915-16, p. 66-93.

C. Ricci, *Tavole storiche dei mosaici di Ravenna*, VIII, *Sant'Apollinare in Classe*, Rome, 1935.

M. Mazzotti, *La basilica di Sant'Apollinare in Classe*, cap. VIII, *I Mosaici*, p. 162-188, Città del Vaticano, 1954.

COLOUR PLATES

THE SO-CALLED MAUSOLEUM OF GALLA PLACIDIA

Plate 5.   THE SO-CALLED MAUSOLEUM OF GALLA PLACIDIA - The Winged Lion: Symbol of the Evangelist Saint Mark ▶

THE BAPTISTERY OF THE CATHEDRAL

Plate 6.   THE BAPTISTERY OF THE CATHEDRAL - Saint Peter ▶

Plate 7.   THE BAPTISTERY OF THE CATHEDRAL - Saint Bartholomew ▶

Plate 8.   THE BAPTISTERY OF THE CATHEDRAL - Saint Thomas   ▶

Plate 10.   THE BAPTISTERY OF THE CATHEDRAL - The Garden of Heaven behind a Grille   ▶

THE ARCHIEPISCOPAL CHAPEL

Plate 13.   THE ARCHIEPISCOPAL CHAPEL - Ornamental Motif with Birds   ▶

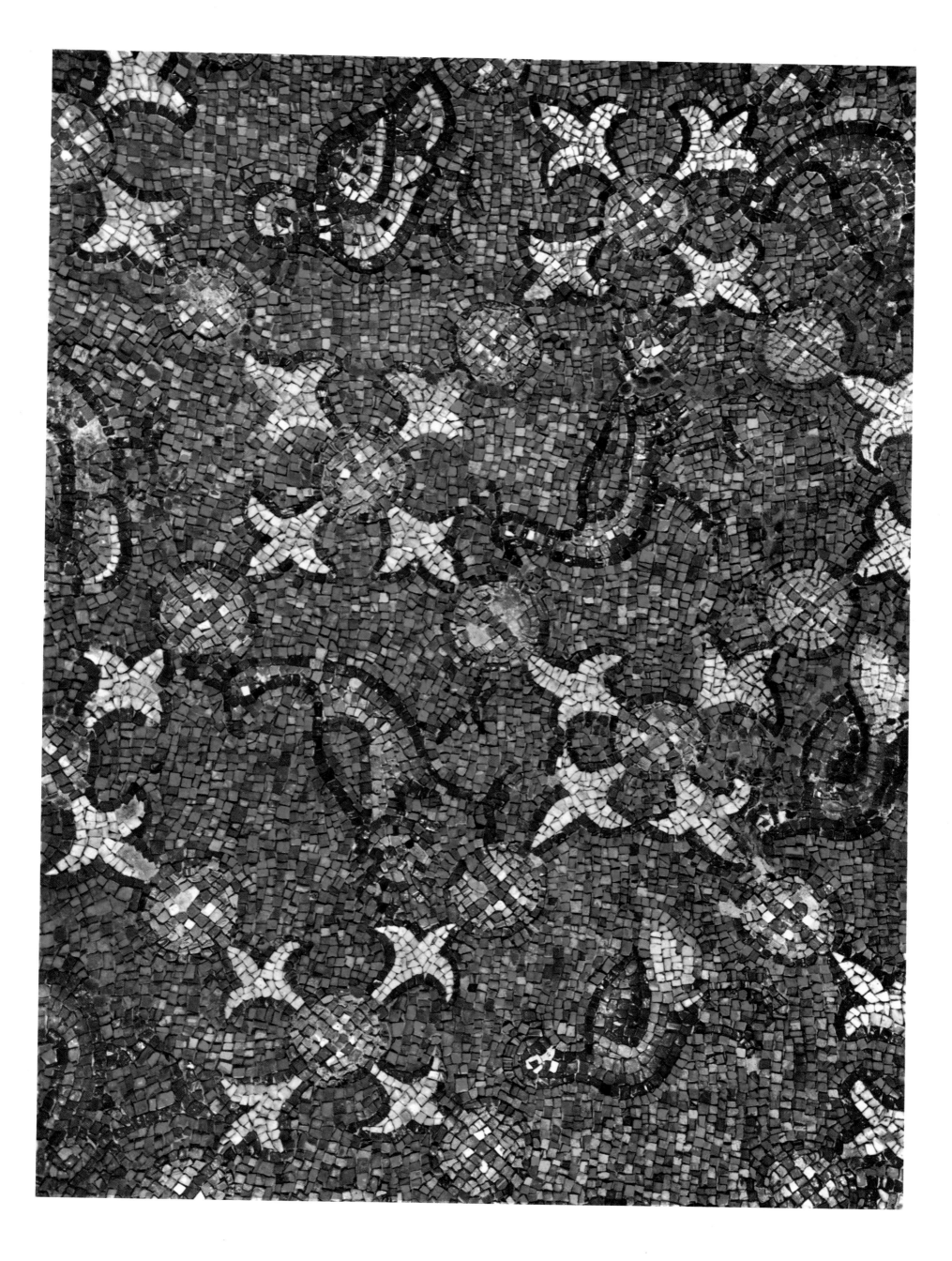

Plate 14. THE ARCHIEPISCOPAL CHAPEL - Christ in Armour ▸

Plate 16.   THE ARCHIEPISCOPAL CHAPEL - Saints Lucy and Cecilia   ▶

THE BAPTISTERY OF THE ARIANS

Plate 17.   THE BAPTISTERY OF THE ARIANS - Cross on a Throne   ▶

Plate 18.   THE BAPTISTERY OF THE ARIANS - Saint Paul   ▶

THE BASILICA OF SANT'APOLLINARE NUOVO

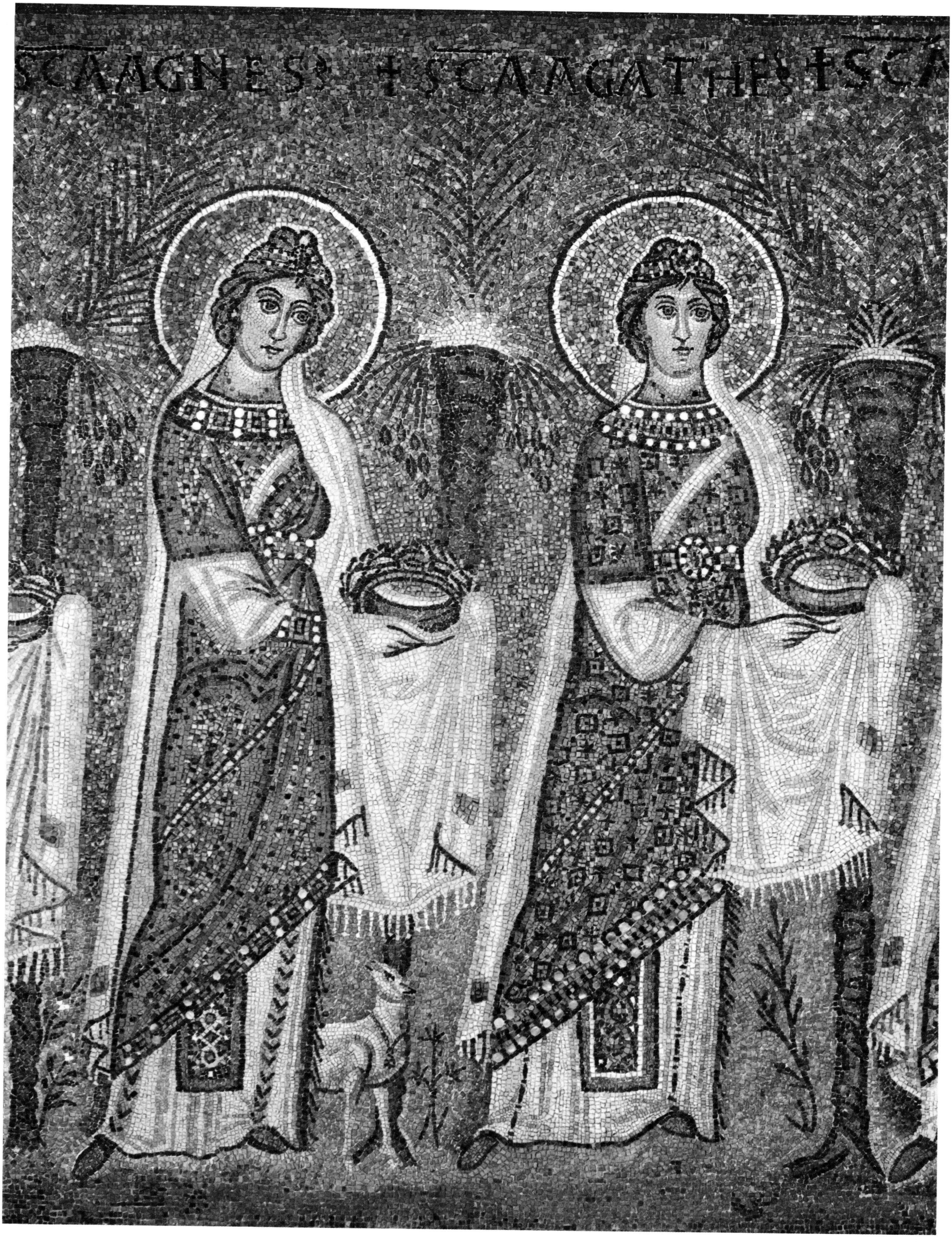
SCA AGNES
+ SCA AGATHE
+ SCA

+SCS BALTHASSAR +SCS MELCHIOR +SCS GASPAR.

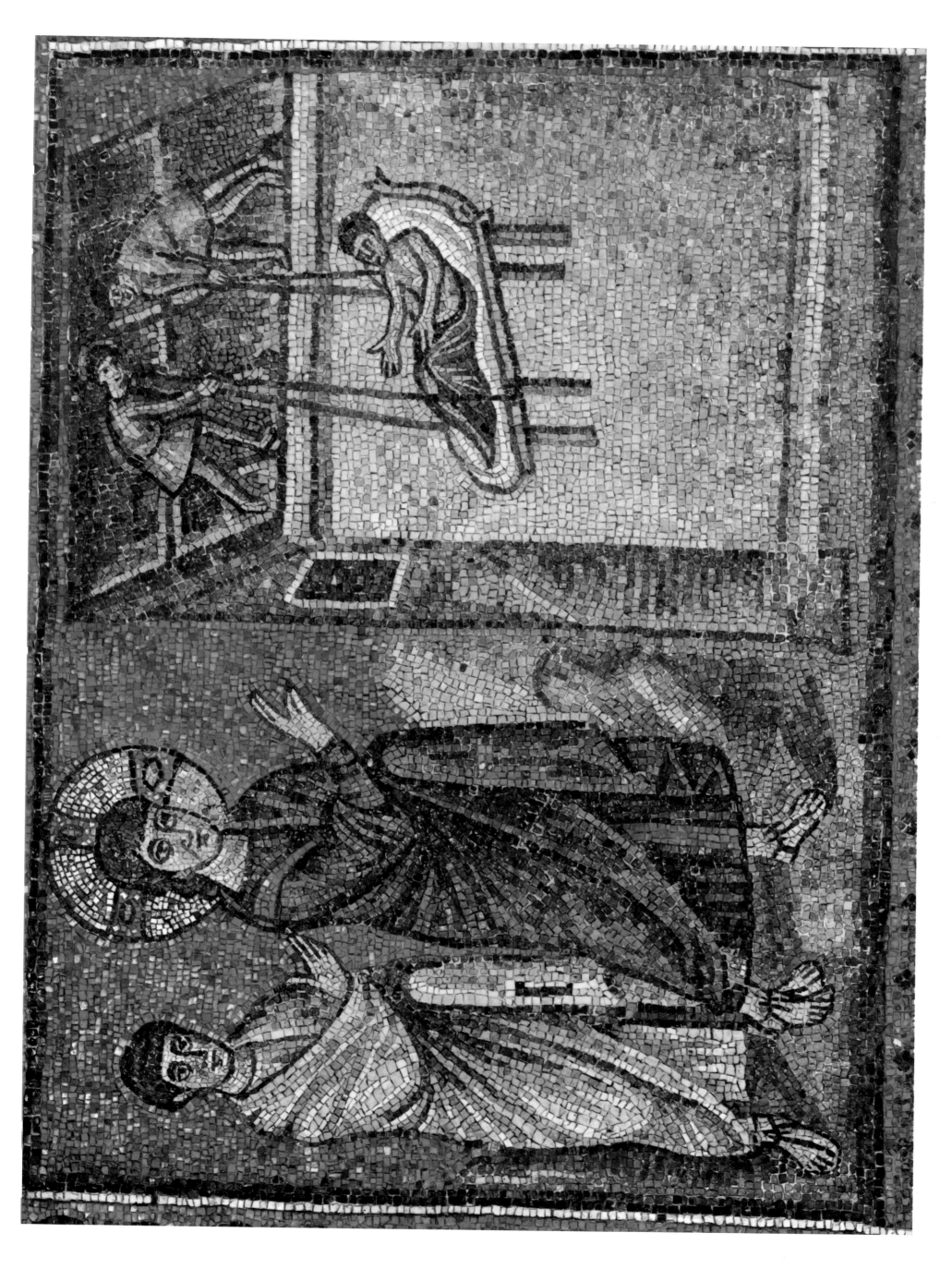

THE CHURCH OF SAN VITALE

MAXIMIANVS·

Plate 28.

THE CHURCH OF SAN VITALE - Justinian Bringing Gifts at the Consecration of the Church

Plate 29.   THE CHURCH OF SAN VITALE - Justinian's Bodyguard, detail   ▶

Plate 30.   THE CHURCH OF SAN VITALE - Justinian, detail   ▶

Plate 31.   THE CHURCH OF SAN VITALE - Bishop Maximian, detail   ▶

Plate 32.   THE CHURCH OF SAN VITALE - Two Prelates, detail   ▶

Plate 33.

THE CHURCH OF SAN VITALE - Theodora Bringing Gifts at the Consecration of the Church

Plate 34.   THE CHURCH OF SAN VITALE - Nobleman Opening the Curtain, detail   ▶

Plate 35.   THE CHURCH OF SAN VITALE - Theodora, detail   ▶

Plate 36.   THE CHURCH OF SAN VITALE - Antonina and her Daughter, detail   ▶

Plate 37.   THE CHURCH OF SAN VITALE - Theodora's Attendants, detail   ▶

Plate 38.   THE CHURCH OF SAN VITALE - Saint Ecclesius   ▶

Plate 39.   THE CHURCH OF SAN VITALE - An Angel, detail   ▶

Plate 40.   THE CHURCH OF SAN VITALE - Peacock, Dove and Flowers, detail   ▶

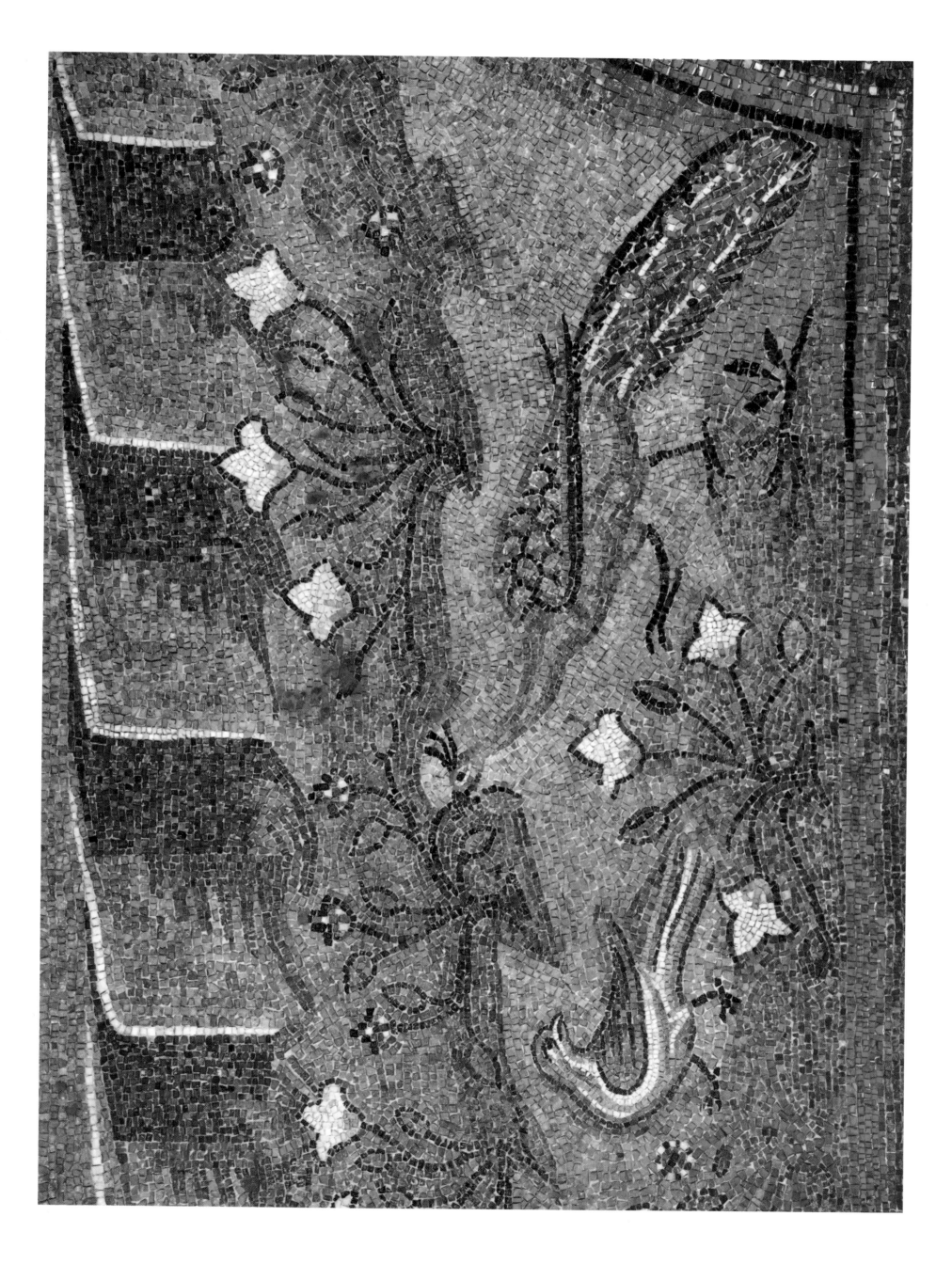

Plate 41.   THE CHURCH OF SAN VITALE - The Sacrifice of Abel, detail   ▶

Plate 42.   THE CHURCH OF SAN VITALE - Moses before the Burning Bush   ▶

Plate 43.   THE CHURCH OF SAN VITALE - Mount Sinai, detail   ▶

THE BASILICA OF SANT'APOLLINARE IN CLASSE

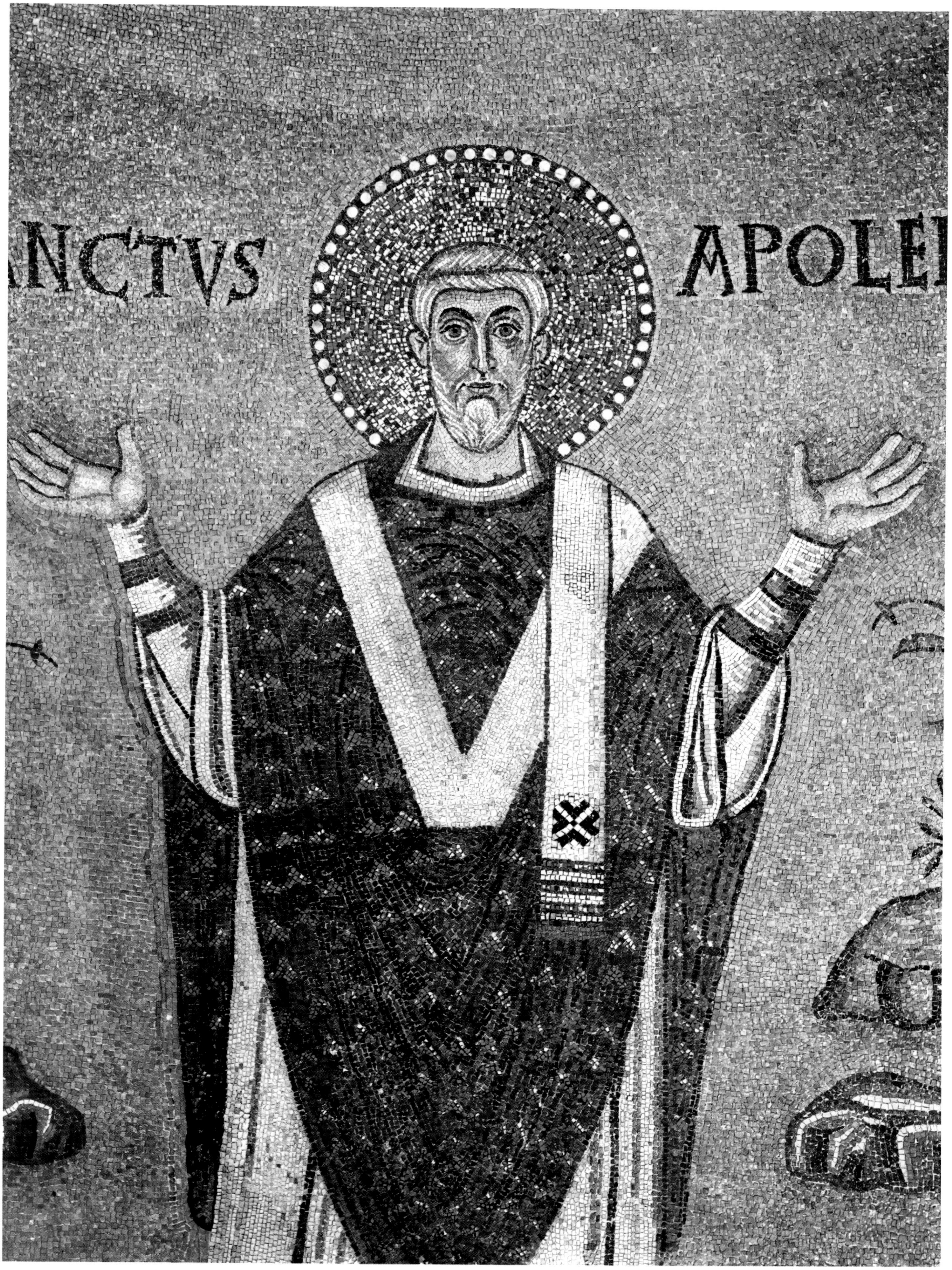
ANCTVS
APOLE

INDEX OF COLOUR PLATES